W9-ABZ-241

Saint Peter's University Library
Withdrawn

AMERICAN EDUCATION

Its Men,

Ideas,

and

Institutions

Advisory Editor

Lawrence A. Cremin
Frederick A. P. Barnard Professor of Education
Teachers College, Columbia University

AMERICAN EDUCATION: *Its Men, Ideas, and Institutions* presents selected works of thought and scholarship that have long been out of print or otherwise unavailable. Inevitably, such works will include particular ideas and doctrines that have been outmoded or superseded by more recent research. Nevertheless, all retain their place in the literature, having influenced educational thought and practice in their own time and having provided the basis for subsequent scholarship.

THE EDUCATION OF GIRLS

IN THE

UNITED STATES

BY

SARA A. BURSTALL

ARNO PRESS & THE NEW YORK TIMES
*New York * 1971*

Reprint Edition 1971 by Arno Press Inc.

American Education:
  Its Men, Ideas, and Institutions - Series II
ISBN for complete set: 0-405-03600-0
See last pages of this volume for titles.

Manufactured in the United States of America

Library of Congress Cataloging in Publication Data

Burstall, Sara Annie, 1859-1939.
   The education of girls in the United States.
   (American education: its men, ideas, and insti-
tutions. Series II)
   Reprint of the 1894 ed.
   Bibliography: p.
   1. Education of women--U.S.
I. Title. II. Series.
LC1752.B9 1971   374.9'73   79-165709
ISBN 0-405-03698-1

THE EDUCATION OF GIRLS

IN THE

UNITED STATES

THE EDUCATION OF GIRLS

IN THE

UNITED STATES

BY

SARA A. BURSTALL

*Scholar of Girton College, Cambridge, and B.A. Univ. of London
Mistress at the North London Collegiate School for Girls*

London
SWAN SONNENSCHEIN & CO
NEW YORK: MACMILLAN & CO
1894

"C'est dans le gouvernement républicain que l'on a besoin de toute la puissance de l'éducation."

MONTESQUIEU, *Esprit des Lois.*

" America is another word for opportunity."

EMERSON.

" We have no established church ; we have established education."

J. G. CROSSWELL (*Harvard*).

TABLE OF CONTENTS

	PAGE
PREFACE, etc.	vii
GENERAL INTRODUCTION	1
CHAPTER I.—ORGANIZATION	10
A. General Outlines	10
Local and Central Boards	11
Finance	14
Teachers and Examinations	16
Kinds of Schools and Relations between them.	17
Superintendents	23
Politics in the Public Schools	26
B. Massachusetts	26
Early School Law	27
Existing System; Towns and School Committees .	30
The State Board	31
Some Notes on the Present Law	33
High Schools: Boston, Cambridge, Brookline .	35
C. The High School Board of Minnesota	38
D. The Universities	41
E. The University of the State of New York . . .	43
CHAPTER II.—HIGH SCHOOLS	46
Organization	47
Daily Routine	50
Home Study	54
Buildings	56
Discipline, marks, etc	61
Examinations; Relations with the Universities .	66
General Remarks	69
CHAPTER III.—PRIVATE SECONDARY SCHOOLS	72
General Remarks	73
Preparation for College	75
Private Boarding Schools	76

PAGE

CHAPTER IV.—METHOD 77
  General Outlines . , ... 77
  The Teaching of Mathematics 81
    „ „ „ History 88
    „ „ „ Science 97

CHAPTER V.—UNIVERSITY EDUCATION FOR WOMEN . . . 105
  General Outlines 106
  Women's Colleges in General 111
    Special Institutions—
      (a) The Harvard Annex 118
      (b) Vassar 123
      (c) Smith 125
      (d) Wellesley 126
      (e) Bryn Mawr 129
      (f) Massachusetts Institute of Technology . 132
      (g) University of Chicago 133

CHAPTER VI.—THE UNIVERSITY OF MICHIGAN . . . 136

CHAPTER VII.—PHYSICAL EDUCATION 146
  General Observations. 146
  The Sargent System at Harvard 148
  The Swedish System, Boston Normal College . . . 150
  Delsartianized Physical Culture 151
    Special Institutions—
    Women's Colleges—
      Vassar 152
      Wellesley 153
      Smith 155
      Bryn Mawr 156
  Physical Training in the Public Schools. . . . 157
  Dress 158
  Music and Elocution 159
  Need of Free Games 159

CHAPTER VIII.—CO-EDUCATION OF BOYS AND GIRLS . . 161

CONCLUSION 167

LIST OF INSTITUTIONS VISITED 176

BIBLIOGRAPHY 183

APPENDIX 191

PREFACE

In view of the growing interest in Secondary Education in the United Kingdom and the important problems awaiting solution, the Gilchrist Trustees decided in the early part of 1893 to send five women teachers to America, for the purpose of studying and reporting upon Secondary Schools for Girls and Training Colleges for Women in different parts of the United States. The Trustees made their intention widely known, and invited the governing bodies of the various women's colleges and associations of teachers to submit to them names of persons specially qualified. Out of the list of able and experienced women teachers thus furnished to them, the Trustees, after careful consideration of the qualifications of the numerous candidates, selected the following five and awarded to each of them a travelling scholarship of £100 to enable them to spend two months in the United States in prosecuting their enquiries :—Miss A. Bramwell, B.Sc. (Lecturer at the Cambridge Training College) ; Miss S. A. Burstall, B.A. (Mistress at the North London Collegiate School for Girls); Miss H. M. Hughes

(Lecturer on Education at University College, Cardiff); Miss M. H. Page (Head Mistress of the Skinners Company's School for Girls, Stamford Hill); and Miss A. Zimmern (Mistress at the High School for Girls, Tunbridge Wells). The five scholars visited America in the summer of 1893, and submitted to the Trustees carefully prepared reports, one of which—viz. that by Miss Burstall—is presented to the public in this volume. The Trustees have aided in the publication of these reports, because they believe that a knowledge of the educational systems and experiments which have been tried in America cannot fail to be of interest and value to those engaged in teaching in the United Kingdom.

R. D. ROBERTS,

Secretary to the Gilchrist
Trustees.

17, VICTORIA STREET,
LONDON, S.W.

INTRODUCTION

In the following pages I have attempted to state the results of an enquiry into Secondary Education and Institutions for the training of women, made by me as one of the Gilchrist Travelling Scholars, during a visit of two months to the chief cities of the United States, in April, May and June, 1893. A list of the cities and institutions visited will be found below.

In order to fit myself for this work, I devoted some time to a course of reading in American educational literature. This is abundant, and while travelling in America, I was able, through the kindness of the various school and college authorities, to form a somewhat wide collection of books and pamphlets dealing with the various aspects of the question ; a bibliography of these and other works read is given below. I have thus been able, to some extent, to understand the aims of American educators, and check the observations I made in the schools themselves. I have also quoted from reports and other writings of Americans in order to put their views before English readers.

The instructions from the Trustees state that the Report should be framed so as to furnish " information or suggestions that may prove useful to those concerned or interested in similar branches of education in the United Kingdom." To do this properly it has been necessary to follow, as far as possible, the example of Mr. Llewellyn Smith, in his Report to the London County Council, and " cover a somewhat wider ground than per-

haps is usual in official reports." I have, therefore,
endeavoured to connect the phenomena of American
education with national characteristics, and with social
and economic conditions, in order that allowance might be
made for any differences between the two countries. I
have also been obliged to give some pages to a general
account of American education before discussing secondary education, for, in the United States, the unity of the
system is such that it would be impossible to understand
part without considering, at least in outline, the whole.
This remark applies especially to the chapter on State
organization; but neither the time nor the resources of
the present writer would allow such minute and thorough
study as in Mr. Llewellyn Smith's classic work.

That which is distant can only be seen in large outline :
those who feel so strong an interest in American education as to desire to examine it more closely and in greater
detail, will find ample information, more particularly of
a statistical character, in the Annual Reports of the
Bureau of Education, and in the circulars published
under its authority : these works are accessible to English readers, particularly through the pedagogic library
of the Teachers' Guild. The great Report drawn up for
the French Government by the State Commission
(headed by M. Buisson), after months of study in
America, and dated 1876, is a mine of information. It
can be consulted at the British Museum. Its general
plan and arrangement somewhat resemble the present
much less complete Report. I am, however, bound to
say that my own scheme was completely drawn up, and
in part carried into execution, before I read M. Buisson's
admirably lucid and most valuable volume. The table
of contents will show the method I have used in attempting to report upon the subject of Secondary Education.
Some introductory observations embody the generaliza-
tions I have been able to form as to the most character-

istic features of American education. The earlier chapters give some account of the organization of the public school system, of the Public High Schools, and of private Secondary Schools. Chapter IV. is devoted to the method of teaching in general, and to the teaching of Mathematics, History, and Science in particular. Chapter V. deals with Women's Colleges, and Chapter VI. with the University of Michigan. Chapter VII. gives an account of Physical Education in the United States, and Chapter VIII. discusses co-education.

The final section, or conclusion, is an attempt to summarise such information as is, in my opinion, most worthy of attention in England. In the Appendix will be found a few statistical tables.

It is difficult, and indeed almost impossible, to express adequately my thanks to those educators in America without whose co-operation my work would have been in vain. Everywhere the credentials from the Gilchrist Educational Trust, and from Dr. J. G. Fitch, procured for me the most kindly welcome, and the most unwearying guidance and help. Even after returning to England I received a considerable number of educational publications ; while, again and again, during my visit, men and women engaged in the full current of professional work turned aside to give me hours of their time in explanations and interviews.

I must, however, endeavour to make some special acknowledgment of the debt I owe to Dr. Harris, the United States Commissioner of Education. The Bureau at Washington was the first institution I visited : there I received most valuable advice from Dr. Harris as to my further course of study. The books and pamphlets placed at my disposal were of the greatest service to me, more particularly his own works, as the following pages show. The statistics are drawn almost entirely from his reports. To his influence I owe my first clear conception of American thought on educational matters, and of the lines along which I should work.

To the authorities of the Universities and Colleges also I wish to express my sincere thanks, more particularly to President Eliot, of Harvard, President Angell, of the University of Michigan, General Francis Walker, President of the Massachusetts Institute of Technology, and to the Presidents and Officers of the Colleges I visited, for their hospitality and help. Dr. James McAlister, of Philadelphia, and Colonel Parker, of Chicago, Mr. J. G. Crosswell and Dr. Leete, of New York, gave me much information and guidance on the more purely educational questions ; while to Professor George Palmer, of Harvard, and Mrs. Alice Freeman Palmer I owe more than I can well say.

No one can be more conscious than the writer of the many shortcomings and faults of the following pages. The subject is one of great difficulty, needing the undivided attention of years—not months—of labour. It has been written in the intervals of professional work by one whose best energies must be devoted to the duties of a teacher. Under such circumstances the writer would plead for some measure of indulgence, especially for possible inaccuracies in matters of detail.

S. A. B.

North London Collegiate School for Girls.

The Education of Girls in the United States.

GENERAL INTRODUCTION.

THE extraordinary enthusiasm for education shown by nearly all classes and sections of the community in the United States is the first fact to be taken into consideration in any discussion of the subject. This feeling, in some sections of the country, rises to the dignity of a conviction—a belief. It shows itself not only in the newspaper press, the reviews, and in the general public interest in educational questions, but in the respect paid to teachers, and even to school houses, and most of all perhaps in the most practical way,—in the enormous sums devoted to educational purposes, both by public bodies and private individuals. To realise this fully, it is necessary to travel in America, to visit the magnificent and costly buildings—occupying often the most important sites of the cities—to know something of the social life of the country, and to study its current literature. It is easy, however, to quote a few illustrations, practical—perhaps mercenary—but of the most common kind.

B

Harvard University at Cambridge has received on the average, for the last twenty years, £80,000 per year in gifts. Last year it received £88,000; the University of Pennsylvania records £40,000 in gifts during the same year. The sums spent by the local authorities on the public school system are also large, as may be seen in the chapters that follow. It may be noted that even in the Western State of Kansas, one half of the taxes levied are for school purposes.

The reasons for this enthusiasm for education may now be given. The first is the democratic constitution of the country: this is well stated in the current Report of the Board of Education of Massachusetts.

"The State depends on the common education of the people as the only cause of that unity of ideas necessary to its continued existence. To produce such an education requires public schools in which the children are organized into a community of persons required to labour together for some common end. In no other way can the young be trained into that social state which prepares them to become a people, controlled in their civil relations by self-imposed rules."

This necessity is well understood in England, and need not therefore be enlarged upon.

The second reason is one which applies only to the United States; it is the immense foreign immigration. The public school is the only security for a homogeneous nation: this matter is referred to constantly by Americans, both in literature and conversation. Of late years the immigration of Southern European and Sclavonic races, often at a lower stage of culture, has made the necessity for education more pressing; only in this way can the children of these varying races and religions become worthy citizens of a united nation. Private and denominational schools are considered only to perpetuate the isolation which already exists among the alien parents of many American-born children. Language is the great instrument of unification; for this reason English is everywhere compulsory in the American public schools, even when it is a foreign tongue to nearly all the children. In some cities, *e.g.*, Cincinnati and Chicago, which have a large German population, local feeling has enforced the teaching of German in addition, but English is still the language of the school. "The mere fact of separate education, especially when promoted by the affluent, tends to the rearing of castes, the creating of a gulf between the rich and the poor, and the laying of foundations for the continuance of those labour troubles that are convulsing this whole land. Great as these mischiefs inevitably are, they will be indefinitely enhanced should we remain a polyglot nation. Language is the great unifier. . . . Without a common language we cannot become a nation. Without the execution of our school laws, we cannot attain to a common language, or at least such attainment will be indefinitely delayed." [1]

In all schools very great attention is paid to

[1] Report of the Board of Education of Massachusetts, 1891–1892.

English; a remarkable illustration of this intense zeal for the language of the nation is the fact that English is the *only* compulsory study at Harvard University.

There is a third reason, much more difficult to explain, and not so generally commented upon as the others.

The great natural wealth of a new country suddenly opened to the conquest and appropriation of mankind, has tended to give material welfare an undue importance in America. Education is held to be the best means to restore the balance, and to preserve the ideal and spiritual elements of human life. Commerce and travel have made Europe familiar with American wealth and materialism; critics here have not fully realised the efforts made in America to elevate and purify the national sentiment by the influence of education. George William Curtis, in his address to the University of the State of New York, alluded to this in language whose dignity befits the subject.[1] "But amid the exultation and coronation of material success, let this University here annually announce in words and deeds the dignity and superiority of the spiritual life, and strengthen itself to resist the insidious invasion of that life by the superb and seductive spirit of material prosperity. . . . The most precious gift of education is not the mastery of sciences, but noble living, generous character, the spiritual delight which springs from familiarity

---

[1] 1890, University Convocation.

with the loftiest ideals of the human mind, the spiritual power which saves every generation from the intoxication of its own success. . . . Agassiz spoke for the scholar in science, when he was besought, for the reward of a fortune, to enter the services of a company, and answered :—' I have no time to make money.' "

This estimate of Education — as a check to materialism—is accountable for a phenomenon in higher education which strikes an English teacher at once, *i.e.*, the tendency to make a subject attractive and simple, and to pay little attention to minute points of scholarship. It is easy to condemn this, and to reproach American schools with superficiality,—such a judgment is itself superficial, since it ignores some elements of the problem. When the boys have to be diverted from the mania for making money, and the girls from the passion for spending it, it is absolutely necessary for the teacher to present learning in its most alluring aspect. What is done may be done thoroughly, but, if it is done at all, it *must* be made enjoyable.

It may be said further, that, as a rule, persons who devote themselves to higher education in America have given up much; the natural gifts and industry required for a man to be a good teacher or professor would probably enable him to make a fortune in business. Thus teachers occupy a position somewhat resembling that of ministers of religion, their work being spiritual, and their reward being in part of an immaterial character.

The public school system in America has three

marked characteristics : it is free, local, and secular. The first comes from the feeling that education is a general public need and must be provided for, not by the parents, but by the public authority; the second is due to the strength of local influences, and the belief in local government and de-centralization; the third is in accordance with the spirit of the American Constitution,[1] and the view of education as a unifying agent in a heterogeneous population. At the same time parents are free to send their children to a private or denominational school should they wish to do so; in no public school is any religious instruction given.[2]

As there is so much feeling for education in America, there is a remarkable degree of *unity*, to an English observer, among the different parts of the educational system.   Although there is a great gap between the secondary schools and the universities, the gap is in some places bridged, and many educators are discussing the best means of filling it up.   Teachers pass with comparative freedom from one kind of work to another.   The prevalence of co-education adds to this unity, and men and women teachers work together much more than is the case in this country. Thus it is impossible to study secondary education for girls, without first studying the educational system as a whole ; public secondary

---

[1] " Congress shall make no law respecting an establishment of religion."   Amendment I.

[2] In many parts of the country Sunday schools are large and successful, and are attended by all classes and by persons of all ages.   They excite much interest and enthusiasm.

schools are under the same authorities and the same laws as the elementary schools.

Not only is there unity, there is an astonishing uniformity over the whole of the United States in organization, methods, courses of study—everything. Some districts and schools are, of course, better than others; some are permeated by a different spirit. But in outward form the uniformity over so large an area, with such absolute local freedom of variation, is extraordinary. The Educational Exhibit at Chicago showed this uniformity in a remarkable degree; the educational literature, reports, school laws, etc., show it also. It is perhaps not too much to say that there is less difference in form between the schools of Boston, Chicago, San Francisco, and Seattle in the State of Washington, than there is between the different girls' high schools in London. The causes of this uniformity may be seen in the chapter on " The Uniformity of American Life," in Mr. Bryce's book.[1] To the influences mentioned there—equality, inter-communication, deference to the will of the majority, newness of the country — may be added the influence of the many teachers' societies and meetings, by which technical knowledge is disseminated, and of that accessibility to new ideas which is so remarkable a feature of the national character. Thus, whatever is considered best tends to become general, and improvement, when it begins, is rapid.

At the present time American educators are dis-

---

[1] Chap. cxii. p. 684.

cussing the problems of secondary education to a remarkable degree. It appears that they are not satisfied with their own system, feeling that it is in some respects deficient, and more particularly that there is not sufficient connection between the secondary schools and the universities. Dr. Nicholas Murray Butler, of New York, writes, " The specific problem in educational organization, that the American people have to deal with at the present time, is the co-ordinating of the secondary to the superior instruction." Professor G. Stanley Hall, of Clarke University, Worcester, Mass., says, " The chief disease to-day of the educational system of America is the isolation between the higher and the lower elements." In the current calendar of Harvard University occurs the following passage, written by President Eliot : " . . . the most pressing educational work in the United States . . . namely, the work of reforming and uplifting secondary education."

A distinguished committee of ten, with President Eliot as chairman, has been recently appointed by the National Educational Association to investigate the courses of study and methods of secondary schools. Its conference took place in December, 1892, and the members have since been engaged in formulating the results. A report has already been issued.

There is one other feature of American education in the present day which cannot be ignored, though its bearing on secondary education is indirect ; it is the spread of what is termed " the New Education " in the elementary schools, *i.e.*, of the cultivation of *power* rather than knowledge on the part of the child. With it may be connected the interest in the principles of Herbart, and the work that has been done in applying these. This takes the form of the "concentration" plan: one or two subjects are taken as the main object of attention, and everything else is related to them. This matter is worthy of further study by English educators.

We can at present only allude to this dawning renaissance. Such a realization of the ideals of the masters Froebel, Pestalozzi, and Herbart, is a sure sign of a great future, when, it may be, in a new land free from the traditions and superstitions of the old, in an atmosphere of freedom and equality, shall be developed a truly scientific system of educational practice, based on the study of child nature, and inspired by the enthusiasm for humanity.

CHAPTER I

ORGANIZATION

A.—*General Outlines*

THE Public School system in the United States is universally a system of local control. The National Government has nothing whatever to do with education. Its powers are, in general, limited to those expressly given to it by the constitution, and education is not included in these.[1]

There are two institutions in Washington of an educational character, depending on the National Government. They are the Bureau of Education and the Smithsonian Institute. The former collects and diffuses information. The latter somewhat resembles the English Royal Society. The National Government also controls the Military School at West Point and the Naval School at Annapolis.

The States of the Union are for many purposes separate commonwealths; each has its own separate school law. This law has two sources: first, the State Constitution, which is enacted directly by the whole people of the State voting at the polls; and second, the Acts passed by the Legislature. We give below[2] a clause from the Constitution of

---

[1] Bryce, chap. iv. pp. 30-31.   [2] *Infra*, p. 28.

Massachusetts.[1] As other examples we may quote the Constitution of Ohio, of 1802, which declares: "Schools, and the means of instruction, shall for ever be encouraged by legislative provision." The Constitution of Michigan, of 1850, devotes a long article to education, ordaining that a system of schools shall be established all over the State, and providing for the government of the State University. Such constitutional provisions are general in their purport. The Acts of the State Legislature are more detailed in character, providing for the organization of local boards, fixing the school age, making education compulsory, etc. In the next section will be found some account of the School Law of Massachusetts, which has special enactments respecting High Schools.

Subject to the provisions of the school law, the schools are controlled by what would be termed in England the School Board of each district. The Boards are elected locally, levy a local rate, build schools, arrange courses of study, appoint and dismiss teachers, etc. As a rule women are eligible as members, and have the school franchise. The members are, we believe, generally paid for the time actually spent by them on school business. In consequence of the diversity of the methods

---

[1] "The true relation of general government to public education throughout the country is not one of dictation or direction of it—not one of interference in any manner with the State and township management—but it should be one of aid encouragement to the educational organizations already established in the several States."—W. T. Harris.

of local government in the different States, it is
extremely difficult to make any general statement
about these Boards.

Some States have School Districts, small adminis-
trative areas, used only for this purpose. This
system does not work well, and the tendency is to
abolish it.[1] In New England, the townships are in
general the units of school organization, and the
township system is being adopted in the West. All
the States of the Union are divided into counties;
these appear in the school organization in many
States, especially in the South. There is often a
county superintendent, and sometimes a county
school tax.

A city,—and this term includes many centres of
population that we should call villages,—forms a
district in itself, having its own City School Board.
These Boards are not always elected directly by the
people, but may be appointed by the mayor, or in
some other way. In Chicago for instance the Mayor
appoints, and the City Council confirm his nomination.[2] Some of the great cities have small local
bodies in each ward, who also take part in the
government of the schools. This is the case in
Philadelphia, where the system acts very badly.
Local Boards as a rule carry on their work by means

---

[1] Report of the Superintendent of Public Instruction, State
of Minnesota, p. 20.

[2] Only one woman sits on this Board at present. The
Mayor endeavoured to appoint another, but the City Council
refused confirmation, because, it is said, a woman has no
political influence.

of committees,—one on High Schools, one on Finance, one on Buildings, etc. American educators are not altogether satisfied with this system of local government of public schools; it introduces "politics," the bane of American local government,[1] into the management of the schools, and thus lowers their efficiency. To this evil influence is attributed the inferiority of the public schools in some of the great cities.[2] Local Boards are often also ignorant, narrow-minded, and parsimonious, especially in the poorer rural districts. American feeling is however so strongly in favour of local government, that no great change is likely to be made. Educators rather seek to improve the school law, which in the more enlightened States is extremely minute, and to strengthen the power and influence of the State Boards of Education, which have been established in many States. These Boards have no power of compulsion over the local bodies; there is, however, often a State school fund which they dispense; they can thus ensure the school law being carried out locally. They collect and diffuse information, and report to the Legislature.

All the States except Delaware have a State Superintendent of Public Instruction, who gives advice, hears appeals, makes reports, licenses teachers, etc. In some States he also has the power of dispensing

---

[1] Bryce, chaps. li. and lii. See also *City School Systems in the United States*, page 15, and the speech of G. W. Curtis, before the National Educational Association, 1891.

[2] Articles in *Forum*, by Dr. Rice, October to June, 1892–3.

the State fund; he is the only official in the American system who can be considered to resemble a Minister of Education.   Further details on this subject may be found in M. Buisson's " *Rapport sur l'Instruction primaire*," and in one of the Bureau of Education Circulars by Dr. Philbrick, late Superintendent of Schools of Boston, Mass.[1]   M. Buisson gives elaborate tables of the organization in different States; it is, however, difficult to reduce the varying systems to any such general form.

Schools are supported almost entirely by local taxation; this, like nearly all direct taxation in the United States, is raised by a property tax of so many thousandths (or mils) on the dollar of valuation, all property possessed by the inhabitants of a district being assessed by the public authority for the purpose of taxation.   It is almost impossible to compare this with the English rate of so many pence in the pound, as that is on rent only.   A clearer estimate may be gathered by noting the amount per child raised by local taxation.   For the United States as a whole, this amount is given as $17·22 (£3 12s. 0d.).   A very wealthy district near Boston, Brookline, raised $35 (£7 6s. 0d.).   A poor township among the hills, Mount Washington, Mass., raises $3·90 (16s.).   The average for Massachusetts is $24·53 (£5 0s. 10d.).   Chicago spends $17·87 per child (£3 14s. 7d.).   A Southern State, West Virginia only $8·87 (£1 16s. 5d.).   Full and elaborate details on this subjects are to be found in

---

[1] See Library of Teachers' Guild.

the Reports of the Commissioners of the Bureau of Education.

Besides the local tax, there is generally a State fund, often the proceeds of the sale of public lands, and often also a State tax. This is distributed by the State authorities to equalize the burden of taxation and provide for poorer districts. The amount and the regulations concerning this fund vary from State to State; some extracts from the last Bureau of Education Report may be of interest. The following passage is summarized from the report:—In the North Atlantic States two per cent. is derived from permanent funds. A State tax is levied on all property in the State, and distributed in proportion to the number of school children. Its object is to equalize the burden of taxation. It is almost without exception devoted to salaries; funds for building and equipment are raised locally. Some States grant an appropriation in bulk from the State treasury. The theory of the State tax has now been adopted by nearly all the States of the Union. State moneys furnish the main support of the country schools of the South. The total sums spent on public education in the whole United States for the year 1889–90 was over 28 million pounds; this was raised from permanent funds, local taxes and State taxes. For the same period the number of pupils receiving elementary instruction is given as $12\frac{1}{2}$ millions in public schools and $1\frac{1}{2}$ millions in private schools. The statistics for secondary education are given in the Appendix.

There is nothing in the American system corresponding to the inspections of English public elementary schools by Her Majesty's Inspectors, nor is there anything resembling the Government grant. Nor are there any great public examinations affecting secondary schools such as the local examinations of the Universities of Oxford and Cambridge, the Matriculation of the University of London, the College of Preceptors' Examinations, etc., etc. At first sight the absence of any such external tests in American High Schools strikes an English observer as the most remarkable difference between us and them. American educators indeed are in general opposed to the examination system, except under special circumstances, and with special safeguards. The writer many times asked if there were any demand for local examination by the Universities, and was always answered in the negative.

The qualifications of teachers for public schools are not subject to any general regulation. Each district and each school committee does as it pleases. The present writer did not study this question, considering that it belonged rather to the subject of the training of teachers.[1]

Male and female teachers are both employed in the public schools, by far the greater number being women; the reason for this is not so much theoretical as practical, the women receiving lower salaries. Principalships are generally held by men, though some primary schools (schools for the youngest children) are under women principals.

---

[1] See *The Training of Teachers in the United States*, by Miss Bramwell and Miss Hughes.

The percentage of male teachers employed has of late years been declining. This is considered an evil; the vigour of men is required, it is said, especially in dealing with boys after 14 years of age.

Another evil is that women teachers do not remain long in the schools, as they marry and leave. This causes continual change and a constant flow of inexperienced teachers into the schools. Full details of the percentage of women teachers in different parts are given in the Bureau of Education Report; it is highest in New England and smallest in the South. The last report of the Bureau gives—Number of teachers, males, 125,602; females, 238,333; total, 363,935. The percentage of male teachers for the whole United States is 34·5. In New Hampshire it is 9·8, and in Massachusetts, 9·9.

The public schools are organized in three grades, Primary, Grammar or intermediate, and High Schools, and are always *free*. Indeed in the United States, the word *public* school always denotes a *free* school, the English sense of the term being entirely strange. Some city systems include kindergartens. In rural districts the schools are generally ungraded, the number of pupils being too few to arrange formal courses of study for each year. In the Appendix will be found a tabular statement, taken from the Report of the Bureau of Education, of the number of pupils receiving instruction in the various schools.

The Primary school takes children of six to nine years of age, who learn the elements of language, number, and, of course, reading and writing.

The Grammar school takes up the Primary school

c

children to the age of fourteen or fifteen, many leaving earlier to go to work. In this grade grammar, arithmetic, geography, literature, and United States history are taught. In the more progressive cities and districts a regular course of manual training, which begins with kindergarten occupations, and goes on to sewing and cooking for girls, and wood carving and iron work for boys, has been introduced of late years. The teaching of science in the common schools is a subject now exciting great interest in America. Much has been done in some centres ; details will be given later.[1] Indeed the enriching of the grammar school curriculum generally is now one of the most burning educational questions of the day. President Eliot of Harvard is the leader of a movement to introduce science, mathematics, and some foreign language into the grammar schools, time being found by improving the methods of teaching in other subjects, and by reducing the time given to arithmetic. As more than 90% of the population receive no further education than that given in the grammar schools, the importance of this reform cannot be overestimated. The grammar school in the higher classes corresponds to some extent with an English Middle School or Higher Grade Board School.

The High School is designed to take pupils at fourteen, fifteen, or sixteen years of age, and, like our English High Schools, fulfil for them two different functions,—either prepare them for the

---

[1] *Infra*, pp. 98–100.

University, or finish their education by giving a broader knowledge and a more thorough training than is possible at an earlier age. It is obvious that this requires bifurcation. In Boston and Cambridge separate High Schools, the English and the Latin, are established,—the latter generally means the school which prepares for College; this custom appears to be spreading. There is also a tendency to establish (for boys at any rate) a third kind of High School,— the Manual Training High School. As a rule boys leave school earlier than girls, in order to take to the practical business of life. Educators hope that by establishing these Manual Training schools they may induce many boys to remain two or three years longer in school, when they will receive not only a practical training, but also a further knowledge of literature, history, and modern languages. In all High Schools there are varied courses, discussion of which will be found in Chapter II.

It is remarkable, however, to note how few young people in proportion to the population attend the High Schools. The statistics for the whole of the United States are given in the Bureau of Education Report as follows:—

96·54 % are receiving elementary education.
2·53 %   „   secondary   „
·93 %   „   higher   „

that is, one pupil in 40 attends a secondary school, and one in 107 a University.

Even in Massachusetts, where education is so advanced, we find a city like Cambridge, with 70,000 inhabitants, and two excellent High Schools, returning only 753 pupils in attendance; Boston, with a population of nearly half a million, has only 3,488 pupils attending the public High School. In other parts of the United States the difference is even more marked; New York, with 1,200,000 inhabitants, has one High School for girls and one for boys, containing 3,000 pupils. [1] In the new city of Seattle, Washington, there are 183 pupils in the High School from a population of 58,000; Cincinnati has 1,503 pupils out of a population of 300,000; Chicago 4,200 with over a million inhabitants. Secondary education is therefore either relatively less important than elsewhere, or is given in other institutions than the public High Schools. The latter is certainly true; it is impossible to say whether the former statement is true or not.

It is thus seen that in the United States the organization of schools does not correspond with the theoretical age of leaving school, as in England, where one set of schools is designed for children leaving school at thirteen, and another for those leaving at sixteen, and the first grade secondary schools for scholars remaining till eighteen years of age or later. The American theory is that all children learn the elements of knowledge in the same way, no matter what their later life may be, and that they all go on together year after year, the only difference being that they drop out of the ranks at different ages. There is nothing in the public school system similar to the English custom

---

[1] Approximately.

of teaching modern languages to the children of the wealthier classes at an early age, or of beginning Latin at eight years of age with boys who are going to the University. There are few educational subjects on which the American experience may be of more use to English education than this question, whether education should be the same for all in the early years, new subjects being introduced as the years of school life increase, or whether, as with us, the whole scheme of work should be made by considering the age at which the pupil must leave school. Such a question should be a matter of educational technique, and is not dependent on civic or political organization, amount of money available for school purposes, or even on social conditions, though these may determine which system is followed. It is probable that in England the comparative fixity of social lines of demarcation, and not a pedagogic opinion as to what is ideally best, has brought about the existing classification of our schools; the modern "educational ladder" of scholarships set athwart those lines has brought before practical teachers the difficulties arising from the difference in the curriculum of a public elementary school, and that of a school preparing for the University, or even of a middle school. In America, on the other hand, no such system, even if educationally the better, could obtain in the public schools. Although social differences do exist, there is very little fixity of social caste. It is impossible to say, for example, at an early period, whether a boy will go to College and enter the ranks of the professions, or whether he may be

SAINT PETER'S COLLEGE LIBRARY
JERSEY CITY, NEW JERSEY 07306

obliged to leave at the age of twelve or fourteen and struggle for bread. Not only are fortunes made quickly, but they are lost easily. It is perhaps hardly necessary to refer to the cases of Presidents whose only regular education was received in the public elementary school; it may be more to our purpose to note that any girl may come in later life to the position of a leader in society, and that educators, in discussing questions of theory, fully allow for this.

Thus the American ideal is that all children should receive the same education, beginning with the absolute minimum, and adding as much as may be during the years of childhood, reserving for the High School such studies as can best be dispensed with from the equipment of the human being as such. It is for this reason that foreign languages are kept for the High School, although such a plan may mean that they are never as well known as they would have been if begun at an early age.[1]

The great advantage of the American system is that promotion is perfectly easy from one grade to another, and that *unity* is established, there being no real distinction between elementary and secondary education, except the age and state of development of the pupil. Such a system is obviously the simplest, and perhaps the ideally best, if secondary as well as elementary education is to be under public control. But it presupposes an absence of

---

[1] Brookline, Mass., is trying the experiment of teaching French, and even Latin, in the grammar school.

those social lines of demarcation which make it difficult of adoption in countries in which the principle of equality does not prevail as completely as it does in the United States.[1]

There is, however, one feature of American school organization which merits in a high degree the attention of all interested in the public control of education ; it is that termed the *Superintendent System*. It is, essentially, the employment by a public Board of an educational specialist, termed Superintendent, who acts as an adviser in technical matters, and supervises the working of the schools. He is to the public educational system what a city architect or engineer is to an English municipality. The Superintendent is always a practical teacher, and is usually a man of long experience and a College graduate. It is our impression that these Superintendents have been as a rule Principals, or chief assistants, of High Schools, Normal Colleges, and the like. We are told that women do hold this office, especially in the smaller towns and school districts of Massachusetts, but we did not meet with any such case, nor hear of the office being held by a woman in any great town. This is not surprising when the work to be done is considered. The Superintendent's salary is generally fixed a little above that of the Principal of the chief High School.[2]

We quote from Dr. Fitch in reference to the

---

[1] Bryce, chap. v. p. 615.
[2] *Examples.* Chicago and Philadelphia, £1,000. Boston, £800. Brookline, Mass., £700. Cambridge, £600.

functions of a Superintendent.[1] " Within his own
domain, whether a State, a county, or a city, he
combines in himself the characters of a minister of
public instruction, an inspector of schools, a licenser
of teachers, and a professor of pedagogy." The
Superintendent visits all the schools under his charge
periodically, and is supposed to know how the teaching is being done.   He may, and often does, examine
the pupils by written tests.   In some cities promotions from grade to grade depend on these examinations.   Serious breaches of discipline are reported to
him, and all cases of expulsion come through his
hands, even when the power of actual expulsion rests
with the Board.

In some cities no teacher can be appointed (except
for the High School) unless she has passed the
Superintendent's examination, or been licensed by
him.   This doubtless tends to check the appointment
of inefficient teachers who may happen to have
political influence.[2]   He can report as to incapacity
in any particular teacher, but we gathered that the
removal of an incompetent teacher was extremely
difficult, and in some cases almost impossible.   The
Superintendent advises teachers as to the best
methods of teaching, and for this purpose often issues
a manual containing hints on the various subjects in
the curriculum, a custom absolutely necessary for
inexperienced and untrained students, who have gone

---

[1] *Notes on American Schools and Training Colleges*, p. 61.
[2] The training and appointment of teachers were not
studied by the writer, but will be found in other Reports.

straight from the High School to teach little children. In addition he regularly holds teachers' meetings, in which he delivers lectures on pedagogy.

The Reports issued by Superintendents are admirable, and are most interesting documents ; they contain not only complete accounts of the schools, but also discussions of educational questions, and extracts from the works of prominent authorities on pedagogy, both in Europe and America.

To give any account of the relations of a Superintendent to his Board is obviously a difficult and delicate matter; the relations of an expert to an elected Board are always delicate and may be difficult. The efficiency of the system of education in a city depends perhaps more on this than on any one thing. We gathered from conversation with persons of experience that, in general, the Boards do defer to the expert on technical questions, such as courses of study, choice of text-books, etc., though the latter offers room for the indirect influence of publishers. When the system works well, the combination of popular control with expert knowledge ensures success, and presents perhaps the best kind of public school system. An example of this may be found in Brookline, Mass., and probably in many other New England cities. But too often political influence brings about the dismissal of an excellent Superintendent ; they in general cannot count upon any long tenure of office, and there is never, we believe, a retiring pension. This uncertainty of course tends to keep out men of high abilities, who can secure more permanent appointments, and very often higher salaries, under private educational corporations, and in the legal or some other profession. In spite of this, however, the enthusiasm for education which is so remarkable a feature of American social life keeps many men of great ability in the position of Superintendents. The writer cannot leave this part of the subject without endeavouring to express her admiration of the combination of high ideals with practical knowledge, of sympathy and professional enthusiasm with business habits and common sense, which characterizes many American educators holding these important posts.

It is difficult, and certainly injudicious, to attempt to draw from the phenomena of American local government of schools any conclusions which can be of use to English educators. The corruption of municipal politics in America is due to special conditions affecting that country. It is worst in the great Eastern cities, with their large foreign immigration. The school system in Boston has been kept " out of politics " by traditional feeling. In New England generally the town system is pure ; the West varies, the educational system of some of the larger cities only being affected. American educators desire earnestly to exclude politics from educational matters, and this will probably be effected at no very distant date by that power of public opinion which, when once aroused, is, in America, an almost irresistible force.

B.—*Massachusetts.*

This State has always had a great influence in educational matters, and is even now in some respects in advance of others. The North-West generally has been colonized from New England; as Mr. Bryce remarks,[1] the emigration has proceeded along the parallels of latitude; and, as the people went westwards, they took their institutions with them. There has also been a direct imitation of New England methods, due largely to the fact that so many educational institutions elsewhere have been, and are, officered by the men and women of New England. Harvard, Yale, Brown, and the other Eastern colleges have also added their influence. It is interesting in this connection to notice how largely the *personnel* of the new Chicago University, which is intended to be the great University of the West, is recruited from Boston, Cambridge, and New Haven.

The educational law of Massachusetts dates from the year 1642, the period of the opening of our Civil War. The General Court or Parliament of the colony then enacted that in every township the local authority should take account of the manner in which parents employed their children, " especially of their ability to read and understand the principles of religion, and the capital laws of the country." Five years later, another act made the support of public schools compulsory, and education universal and free. This law of 1647 is naturally regarded with pride by the people of Massachusetts, and is frequently alluded to; the official pamphlet on the public statutes relating to education declares it to be " the first law of the kind ever passed by any

---

[1] Vol. ii. page 302.

community of persons, or by any state." It stands
as follows :—

" ORDINANCE OF 1647."

"It being one chiefe object of that ould deluder, Satan, to
keepe men from the knowledge of the Scriptures, as in former
times by keeping them in an unknowne tongue, so in these
latter times by persuading from the use of tongues, that so
at least the true sence and meaning of the originall might be
clouded by false glosses of saint-seeming deceivers, that learning may not be buried in the grave of our fathers in the
Church and Commonwealth, the Lord assisting our endea-
vours : It is therefore ordered that every township in this
jurisdiction, after the Lord hath increased them to the number of fifty householders, shall then forthwith appoint one
within their towne to teach all such children as shall resort
to him to write and reade. . . . And it is further ordered
that where any towne shall increase to the number of 100
families or householders, they shall set up a grammar
schoole, the Master thereof being able to instruct youth so
farr as they may be fitted for the university."

The third paragraph deals with secondary education. The University had already been founded
at Cambridge, by the law of 1637, and had received
John Harvard's name. The State constitution
adopted in 1780 contains the following provision,
which expresses the American view of the need of
education as well, perhaps, as any concise statement
could :—

" THE CONSTITUTION OF MASSACHUSETTS, 1780."

"Wisdom and knowledge, as well as virtue, diffused generally among the body of the people, being necessary for the
preservation of their rights and liberties, and as these depend
on spreading the opportunities and advantages of education
in the various parts of the country, and among the different
orders of the people, it shall be the duty of the legislatures
and magistrates, in all future periods of the Commonwealth,

to cherish the interest of literature and the sciences and all seminaries of them, especially the University of Cambridge, public schools and grammar schools in the towns; to encourage private societies and public institutions, by rewards and immunities for the promotion of agriculture, arts, sciences, commerce, trades, manufactures, and a natural history of the country; to countenance and inculcate the principles of humanity, and general benevolence public and private, charity, industry, and frugality, honesty and punctuality in all their dealings; sincerity, good humour, and all social affections and generous sentiments among the people."

An amendment to the Constitution adopted in 1855, declares that no public money shall be used for sectarian schools.

The later history of education in Massachusetts during the eighteenth and part of the nineteenth century is full of interest, especially the part relating to the work of Horace Mann, between 1837 and 1850, in building up a centralized system, and in introducing normal schools. In recognition of his work, and of the importance of education to the Commonwealth, his statue is one of two standing on the steps of the historic Boston State House. It would be, however, beyond the limits of the present subject to enter into the details of the evolution of the existing system.[1] It is our business rather to describe the system as it stands, noticing especially the parts relating to secondary education.

The great merit of the Massachusetts organization is its combination of local self-government and cen-

---

[1] See Boone, *Education in the United States*, p. 103. G. H. Martin, *Brief Historical Sketch of the Mass. Public School System*, Boston, 1893.

tralized control. The first principle acts through the
township system ; the second through the State
Board of Education. Subject to the provisions of
the general school law, details of which are given
later, the Towns (townships), the lineal descendants
of the primitive Teutonic communities, provide the
schools and govern them by means of a school committee, elected in a town meeting, one-third being
chosen every year. Their powers and duties are as
follows :—

"The school committee has the general charge and superintendence of all the public schools of a city or town. It
establishes courses of study, selects text books, directs how
schools shall be organized, how many schools shall be kept,
what shall be the qualification for admission to the schools,
the age at which children may enter, and the age to which
they may continue ; and has power to regulate the system of
classification and distribution of pupils. It selects and con-
tracts with the teachers of the public schools, ascertains by
examination and otherwise their qualifications for teaching,
and their capacity for the government of schools ; and issues
certificates of character and acquirements. It dismisses
teachers with or without cause stated." [1]

The members receive payment for the time they
actually give to school work.

There are 352 Towns (townships), including 28
cities, and varying from wealthy suburban communities like Brookline, to poor and lonely moun-
tain or sea-coast districts, where the means of the
population are inadequate to provide good schools
without external aid. Each Town is independent,
and might vary considerably from its neighbours.

---

[1] Official Abstract, Chicago Exhibition.

But the Massachusetts State law is so detailed, there are so many provisions to induce the Towns to conform to the best methods in education, that, as a matter of fact, there is a high degree of uniformity, This is largely the work of the State Board of Education established in 1837 ; it is remarkable as having little direct control, its functions being chiefly advisory. But its work has nevertheless been of the greatest value in perfecting and developing the Massachusetts system,[1] and American educators speak highly of it. It consists of eight members (each holding office for eight years), appointed by the Governor, and of the Governor and Lieutenant-Governor, *ex officio.* Among the number of those who have served on the Board are, to quote names well-known in England, Horace Mann, Phillips Brooks, Thomas Wentworth Higginson, and Francis A. Walker. The existing Board includes two women, one being the late head of Wellesley College, Mrs. Alice Freeman Palmer. Such a Board is entirely detached from politics ; this quality is, according to Americans themselves, a rare virtue in a public body. The members serve without any payment.

The Board has " the general management of all the normal schools of the State, and directs and supervises the education of the deaf, the blind, and the feeble-minded, that are educated at the expense of the State." It prescribes the form of registers to be kept in the schools, and through its Secretary,

---

[1] *Mass. Board of Education Report.*

a paid official, collects statistical and other information (the law requires private schools to furnish
returns according to a specified form), and diffuses
it through the Commonwealth.

The Board presents annually to the Legislature
a Report,—"containing a printed abstract of the
said returns (from the schools), a detailed report of
all the doings of the Board, with such observations
upon the condition and efficiency of the system of
popular education, and such suggestions as to the
most practical means of improving and extending
it, as the experience and reflection of the Board
dictate." [1] This has influenced the course of legislation.

The Board also holds in trust the State fund for
educational purposes, arising in great part from the
sale of public lands. The income from this is
divided into two parts; one moiety supports the
normal schools, pays the expenses of the Board,
salary of Secretary, etc., the surplus, if any, going
to the capital account. The other half is divided
by the Board among the poorer Towns, according to
certain regulations. This arrangement is obviously
one of very great importance, tending as it does to
enable poor districts to support such schools as their
own unaided efforts would never enable them to
enjoy.

The Secretary and Treasurer of the Board act
as commissioners to invest and manage the fund.
Only Towns whose valuation is below a certain

---

[1] Official Abstract, Chicago Exhibition.

amount are eligible to receive aid from the State fund. They must also comply with all the laws as to keeping schools open for a certain number of weeks in the year, etc., etc., and must raise by taxation at least a sum of $3 (12*s.*), per person between 5 and 15 years of age, in the district, for current school expenses. It is thus seen that the State aid is meant to encourage local effort, and not to supersede it.

Another arrangement has lately come into force to encourage small and poor Towns and cities to unite to pay for a Superintendent, who shall supervise the schools, instead of having the work done by the school committees, who do not, as a rule, consist of persons specially skilled in education. If the Towns concerned vote in town-meeting to adopt the provisions of the new law, form a union, and raise jointly $750 (£150), as salary for a superintendent, the Commonwealth will then grant from the State treasury a warrant for $1250 (£250), of which $750 (£150) shall go to the salary of the superintendent, and the rest to the increase of the teachers' salaries. This provision has been largely adopted, 121 Towns having united for the purpose of supervision. The employment of skilled superintendence is considered by American educators to be one of the most useful methods of improving the schools of a district. In the whole State 350 cities and Towns have skilled supervision of schools, employing 135 superintendents.

The work of the Secretary of the Board of Education is so important a part of the action for good

of the State system of Massachusetts, that it requires a special note.   Besides the work of collecting
and diffusing statistical and other information above
referred to—in itself a most valuable function, as
any one who reads the Annual Reports of the Board
may ascertain—the secretary and his agents visit
the several towns and cities for the purpose of holding teachers' and other educational meetings, and
often give lectures on pedagogics at the Teachers'
Institutes, which are meetings under the State
law for professional instruction.   From 20 to 25 of
these are held every year, and they are attended by
about 2,000 teachers annually.   The secretary also
suggests to the Board and to the Legislature im-
provements in the present system, and in every
possible manner arouses and guides public sentiment
in relation to the practical interests of education.

Besides the ordinary schools, high, grammar,
primary, and in some places kindergarten, the law
requires evening schools to be maintained, and to be
attended by young persons at work, who do not
know how to write in the English language.   There
are 255 such schools; every city of 50,000 inhabitants is also required to maintain an Evening High
School.   There is a compulsory attendance law, enforced more or less thoroughly according to local
influences.   Several counties (Massachusetts is
divided into 14 counties), and the City of Boston,
support Truant Schools.

The free text-book system has been adopted by
law (1884) in Massachusetts, each school committee
purchasing the books, and lending them to the

pupils ; it is declared to be an unqualified success. Any Town may also pay for the conveyance of pupils to school; this is declared by the secretary of the Board and other persons of experience to be an excellent measure, enabling rural and other districts to concentrate their resources.

An extremely important provision is that enforcing sanitary requirements on *all* schools, public or private, and directing the sanitary inspector, and the local boards of health to ensure the observation of the law.

We have already quoted the law of 1647, requiring the establishment of a grammar school in Towns of over 100 families. This is of course now obsolete ; its place is taken by the law of 1868, as follows :—

" Every town may, and every town containing 500 families or householders shall . . . maintain a High School to be kept by a master of competent ability and good morals, who, in addition to the branches of learning before mentioned, shall give instruction in general history, book-keeping, surveying, geometry, natural philosophy, chemistry, botany, the civil polity of this commonwealth and of the United States, and the Latin language. Such High School shall be kept for the benefit of all the inhabitants of the town, ten months at least, exclusive of vacation, in each year. . . . And in every town containing 4,000 inhabitants, the teacher or teachers of the schools required by this section shall, in addition to the branches of instruction before required, be competent to give instruction in the Greek and French languages, astronomy, geology, rhetoric, logic, intellectual and moral science, and political economy."

164 cities and Towns are required to maintain High Schools, 223 cities and Towns actually do maintain them ; there are now altogether 245 High Schools in

the State, containing 27,482 pupils, and employing 904 teachers. Any Town not required to maintain a High School may pay for the tuition of a child who attends the High School of another Town or city ; two small Towns may unite to form a Union High School District, and have a school between them. In several Towns secondary instruction is provided for those students who would otherwise be in High Schools, by the Town's paying for their tuition in academies.

The public High Schools of Massachusetts have a distinguished reputation ; they prepare largely for College, much more so than the High Schools of the Middle States. The town of Concord has 10% of its children enrolled in the High School. We visited the High Schools of two cities, Boston and Cambridge, and of one Town, Brookline; we shall therefore proceed to give some details concerning these.

Boston has ten High Schools—two for boys, the Latin and the English ; two, corresponding to these, for girls, and six mixed High Schools, belonging to districts recently incorporated. The Girls' English High School was established in 1826 ; public sentiment was, however, against it, and it was abolished, to be, however, revived at a later date. The Girls' Latin School was established in 1878. We should state that, in Boston, the age of admission to the Latin School is low (twelve to thirteen years of age), the course there being five or six, and sometimes even seven, years in length.

Cambridge, a city of 70,000 inhabitants, adjoining Boston, has two public High Schools ; one, the Latin, for boys and girls, prepares for College, and the other, the English, is for those desiring a general education. There is a third, partly supported by the munificence of a citizen, for manual training (boys only). All have admirable buildings, well situated, beautiful, and perfectly adapted to their purpose. Reference is made to these schools elsewhere ; it is enough to say here that their standing is worthy of the intellectual reputation of the city to which they belong.

Brookline is a suburban district (population about 7,000) near Boston, one of the primitive communities or Towns, governing itself still by a town-meeting or primary assembly, but remarkable for its assimilation of all that is best in modern municipal life. Its schools are deservedly famous for their excellence, the wealth and public spirit of the inhabitants having provided an almost ideal equipment, both in material and *personnel*. The system is complete in itself, from the Kindergarten to the High School, the latter preparing for College,[1] and at the same time being closely related to the lower schools. Children of all classes attend the public schools, which are, of course, co-educational, and private schools hardly exist in the township. Brookline is perhaps the best example of the Massachusetts system of organization ; and the excellence of its schools tends to prove that local government, when administered by cultivated and patriotic citizens, is the best method of school management.

It is almost impossible to convey in words an impression of the admirable character of these Brookline

---

[1] 45% of the High School pupils prepare for College.

schools; they must be visited and studied, and the work done in them examined. Reference is made in the following chapters to details of the work,[1] and a table of statistics is given in the Appendix. The reports, courses of study, programmes and syllabuses issued by the Superintendent of the School Committee are full of instruction, and might afford useful suggestions to English teachers : every visitor to America who is interested in education ought to go to Brookline, whatever else may be omitted. This New England Town may indeed be said to afford a standard of what a complete system of public education should be ; the most bitter opponent of public control of education would find it difficult to maintain his opinion after visiting its schools and studying its documents.[2] The conditions for such excellence—an enlightened community, the New England enthusiasm for education, wealth, and public spirit—do not often co-exist ; in Brookline they *are* found in combination, and the result might be a lesson to English educators, even, perhaps, to English statesmen.

C.—*The High School Board of the State of Minnesota.*

This State, which has been largely colonized from New England, and which contains a very large proportion of Scandinavians, has an excellent public school system. The schools of Minneapolis, its capital, are highly praised by Dr. Rice in his articles

---

[1] See Chap. IV. pp. 92, 95, 101, and the Index.

[2] For an account of Brookline, see *New England Magazine* for August, 1893.

in *The Forum*. We much regret not having been able to visit its magnificent High School and that of St. Paul. We were, however, able to gain some information in Chicago from persons who had lived in Minnesota, more particularly the Professor of History at the University, and the Superintendent of the State Exhibit at the Exhibition. Through their kindness we obtained a complete set of the State publications on education, and carefully examined the work sent to Chicago by the schools.

The State possesses a unique feature in its organization in what is known as the High School Board. Its objects are to bridge over the gulf which too often exists in America between the Universities and the public High Schools, and to encourage the poorer districts to provide for secondary education. This Board consists of three members, the Governor of the State, the Superintendent of Public Instruction, and the President of the State University.

The law, which dates from 1881, may be summarized as follows:—The Board receives applications for aid from any properly organized free public school in the State, admitting students of either sex ; and, after being satisfied that the school is working properly, grants a sum of $400 (£80) annually from the State treasury. The conditions which the Board by law requires are, first, that there shall be in the school regular courses of study in preparation for the University of Minnesota, and, second, that the school shall be inspected and approved periodically by members of the Board, or by its agents.

The Board classifies the High Schools into three divisions, according to their excellence, not as measured by the examination results of their pupils, but by their arrangements for complete courses of study, provisions for laboratory work, and for libraries. According to recent statistics, there are 19 in the first class, 30 in the second, and 20 in the third; total, 69 schools, containing 4,290 pupils. This Board has already, according to the testimony of persons of experience, worked wonders. The classification of the schools appeals to that local feeling and rivalry between one city and another, which are so strong in America. Further, pupils who have satisfactorily passed through the course of study of schools of the First Class, are admitted to the State University without further examination. It should be noted that, in accordance with the law quoted above, an inspector appointed by the Board, who is always a practical teacher, visits the High Schools every year, and makes an elaborate report upon them.

There is also a system of State local examinations for pupils in High Schools who may enter for a few subjects each year, and receive a diploma under the seal of the State, after passing a certain number of subjects. These students must go through four years' regular work in an approved High School in order to obtain the diploma.

The State Superintendent of Public Instruction declares that "no department of the public school system is better supported by public sentiment, and none is rendering more appreciable results in education than the State High Schools."[1]

One interesting result of the system is that many boys from the High Schools enter the University, take the course in Liberal Arts, and then go into business. A large number of the teachers in these schools are also graduates of the State University, the High School Board having power to insist upon teachers being properly qualified according to their requirements.

D.—*The Universities.*

In America these institutions stand apart from the State system of public education. They do not have, as in England, a wide influence on secondary education by any general system of local examinations. (We shall explain later the modifications necessary to make these statements absolutely correct.) They have, however, an indefinite influence on education in the public schools, through the personal prestige of their great men, such as the present head of Harvard, President Eliot, whose opinions carry weight everywhere among teachers. They also affect the curricula of the secondary schools by the requirements of the matriculation examinations.

But they do not seem to be as closely connected with secondary education as in England;[2] the ten-

---

[1] Report of Superintendent for 1891–2.

[2] W. T. Harris, in *The Place of University Extension in American Education*, says: "Secondary education developed not on the basis of the university but on that of the elementary school. The course of study in these institutions

dency, however, is to bring the Universities into closer relation with education in general. According to President Gilman, of Johns Hopkins, there are four kinds of Universities in the United States.[1] The first is the College University, of which Harvard is a type; this is often of colonial foundation,[2] and may have received State aid in the past. Many of these were founded by ecclesiastical bodies, and some are still more or less denominational. None of the greater ones are as yet open to women.

The second is the privately endowed University, such as Cornell, Ithaca, N.Y.; Johns Hopkins, Baltimore; and the new University of Chicago. Some of these have been founded by one individual whose name they perpetuate; they comprise some of the wealthiest, best equipped, and most efficient institutions. Some are open to women, some are not; the best women's colleges might be included in this class. They resemble the first class in their legal status as independent corporations, governed by their own Boards, and generally chartered under the laws of the State in which they are situated.

The third class consists of the State Universities; these have been founded by the States' Legislatures,

---

has been under the control of men educated only on elementary methods. . . . Arrested development is the result and mechanical device. . . . It produces a flippant, self-conceited frame of mind. . . . Only one in 500 of the population is now enrolled in schools for higher instruction." —P. 8.

[1] *Cyclopædia of Political Science.* Article, "Universities."
[2] Harvard, 1637. Yale, 1701. Columbia, N.Y., 1754.

are governed by Regents elected by the people, or nominated by the Legislature or Governor, and are supported partly by a State tax, and partly by the funds arising from appropriations of lands to educational purposes by the Federal Government, when the States were themselves created. None of the original thirteen States have State Universities; these occur in all the Western and in some of the Southern States. They are open to women, and are, as State institutions, wholly undenominational, and, in accordance with the Constitution, secular. The most important of these, on which indeed many of the others appear to have been modelled, is the University of Michigan. As this has many features of interest in connection with the present inquiry, and as it is not well known in England, we shall devote a separate chapter to some account of it. Its organization will be there described. The fourth class has but one representative, the University of the State of New York. Its chief work is examination; it is not a teaching university at all. It has, however, special relations with secondary education; a further account of it is therefore given.

E.—*The University of the State of New York.*

This body is an interesting example of an attempt to unify the various institutions for higher education, in the great and populous State of New York, and to raise the standard of such education by the controlling influence of a centralized organization. It consists nominally of all colleges and academies having State charters: these have, however, no

voice in its government; the University is really a
State Bureau of Administration, governed by a
Board, known as "the Regents." They are twenty-
three in number :—the Governor, Lieutenant-Gover-
nor, Secretary of State, and Superintendent of Public
Instruction of the State of New York (*ex officio*),
with nineteen elective Regents who are chosen by
the Legislature as the Senators for the National
Congress are. This body is really, in fact, the
University.[1] The nineteen chairs have been occu-
pied by some of the most eminent citizens of New
York. The University dates from the period of the
Revolution, 1787; it was formed largely under
French influence, but it had very little effect or
influence until the last few years.

Its powers are as follows :—The Regents have
power to incorporate, and to alter or repeal the
Charters of Colleges, Academies, Libraries, Museums,
or other educational institutions belonging to the
University; to distribute to them all funds granted
by the State for their use, to inspect their workings,
and to require annual reports under oath of their
presiding officers; to establish examinations as to
attainments in learning, and to confer on successful
candidates suitable certificates and degrees. They
thus have power to do what the University of
London does, but as yet they only exercise this
power to grant Medical Degrees; the institutions
themselves grant their own degrees in their own

---

[1] Among the Regents are Chauncey M. Depew and Whitelaw
Reid ; George Wm. Curtis was Chancellor up to his death.

fashion. The Regents have, however, established local examinations in the secondary schools, the certificate of which is recognised for admission to the College, and is required from all law and medical students. These examinations cover 68 subjects, and necessitate more than 500,000 examination papers yearly; there are 390 secondary schools taking these examinations. The 86 Colleges included in the University do not, of course, enter for them. The Regents apportion annually an Academic fund of $106,000 (£21,200); part for buying books and apparatus for Academies and High Schools, and the balance on the basis of attendance and the Regents' examinations. They are also trustees of the State Library and State Museum, and have a special organization for assisting cities and villages to obtain free libraries. Furthermore they have taken up the work of University Extension.

The University holds a yearly Convocation at Albany, when the teachers and officers of the Colleges and Academies meet to confer on questions of secondary and higher education. The Regents have also established a property qualification for new institutions desiring charters of incorporation; they thus hope to check the multiplication of poor and insufficiently equipped colleges and academies. The work of the University will doubtless extend and become more important as years go on; it is an interesting example of the necessity for those central controlling and supervising bodies in the public education system, which are a marked feature of the most progressive States of America.

CHAPTER II.

IN what follows we refer to the public High
Schools, although the private schools resemble
these to a much greater extent than might be expected. The general age of entrance is 15 to 16 for
pupils entering from the grammar schools of the
city; some come at an earlier age, but few, if any,
later. The certificate from the grammar school,
or an equivalent entrance examination, is required
before admission. This simplifies the work of the
High School, for some subjects can be omitted from
its curriculum as having been sufficiently studied in
the lower school. Arithmetic, grammar, geography,
and United States history in its elementary parts,
are the chief of these. This stratification of subjects is one of the greatest advantages of the public
school system; it enables the High School to devote
considerable time to advanced work, and thus to
avoid the waste of energy caused by studying many
things at once.

The organization of American High Schools is
also much simpler than that customary in England.
The pupils are arranged in years, the year beginning in September; admissions at other times are
only allowed if the applicant can produce evidence,

by examination or certificate, of being fit to take up the class work at the proper point. As a rule the pupils go regularly together to the next year's work; the backward ones either lose a year, and go over the course again, or leave school. We imagine the latter is the more usual alternative. On completion of the prescribed course—in general one of three or four years—a diploma of graduation is given. The occasion for this is often one of some ceremony, girls wearing a special dress, the best pupils of the year reciting addresses, etc.; it takes, indeed, the place of the English distribution of prizes.

Most High Schools have several courses of study, one of which must be chosen when the student enters. There seems to be little provision for change, probably because there is little demand for it. We give in the Appendix details of the courses in some typical schools. One is generally a commercial course, which takes two years; the course preparing for College takes four years. Many girls choose an English course. Boys in some cities take a course of three years for engineering. As stated above, some cities have separate schools for the various courses. The Manual Training High Schools for boys in Philadelphia and Cambridge, Mass., seemed to the writer worthy of special study, but as they do not concern girls, they are beyond the limits of the present inquiry. The school committee of Boston has decided to open a Mechanic Arts High School for Boys, the land to cost £10,000 and the building £24,000. Their report states: "For the first time in Boston, the boy who wishes to enter the industrial world will have the same opportunities given him for preparation, at the public expense, as have been given so long to those who wish to prepare for a business or professional life."

Many pupils leave before graduation, boys especially. This is due to the attraction of practical life. In a mixed school the excess of the number of girls over that of boys is very striking, in what an Englishman would call the " higher forms." The word *form* is, however, not used ; the year is spoken of as a *class*. The class divides for lessons, according to the subjects taken by the individual members.

When a school is very large the class for one year may contain 200 or more. It follows, then, that all who learn the same subject cannot be taught together ; they are therefore divided into sections, and the teacher repeats her lesson. Each teacher takes but one or two subjects. All the pupils are, however, kept parallel in their work. In an English school the differences between pupils would soon be noticed by the teacher, and, after a few lessons, the class would be re-arranged into different sections, the brighter pupils pushed on faster, while the duller ones would receive more explanation of difficulties. We found no trace of such a gradation in even the best public High Schools ; the whole year went on at the same pace, even when the numbers were so large as to require teaching in sections. We were informed by the superintendent of one city that to go further with one set of pupils than with another, if they were both doing the same course and belonged to the same year, would be considered unfair ; it would give the diploma of graduation on easier terms to one pupil than to another, for one would have gone through more algebra, say, or Cicero, than another. This objection was, we think, a sound one according to the American system, in which stress is laid, not on examinations, as with us, but on going through a certain amount of work in the classroom.

Nevertheless, English teachers will feel that to keep a large number working at the same rate, in an advanced subject like mathematics, must mean either that some do not understand what they are learning, or that those with special ability do not make the progress they might ; the latter is probably the case. An American teacher would say this did not matter ; such a boy or girl would go to College and elect to work at advanced mathematics there, and might even go on to post-graduate work. Besides, they might add, " The bright student can get on any way." It should be remembered that there are in America very few open scholarships at the colleges to be won by *competition*. A student of limited means can always get help, in one form or another, but competition has nothing to do with gaining such aid. It is not, therefore, necessary to look out early for the most gifted boys and girls, to train them to reach the scholarship standard, and the school is not judged by the number of College scholarships its pupils obtain.

The result of this difference between American and English High Schools is that there is not, there at the top of the school, a small number of gifted boys or girls doing really advanced work in one or two

E

subjects. It might be said, then, that the standard there must be lower than with us. Such a judgment would be both true and false : true as regards the few, but probably false as regards the many. Owing to the small number of subjects studied, in comparison with those in an ordinary good English High School for girls, a greater number appear to reach a fair standard than with us. In other words, a larger percentage of girls read the sixth book of Euclid there than here, though our best girls read more advanced mathematics, and take subjects which in America are confined to Colleges. The same rule probably applies to other subjects.

The daily routine of an American public High School is confined to the morning only ; the hours are generally from 9 to 1.30. Some schools in small cities begin at 8.30, some go on till 2. There is always a period of rest in the middle of the morning, termed " recess," twenty-five to thirty minutes in length. During this time the pupils have lunch, some returning to their homes, but the majority, especially in large cities, either bringing what they require or purchasing it at school. The schools vary considerably as to the custom of a general assembly before the beginning of the morning's work. In some cities public sentiment is opposed to any religious ceremony in schools ; but in such places pupils are called together for literary exercises, etc., once a week, or oftener. Even in schools where religious exercises are allowed, they often do not take place every day according to the English custom, but once or twice a week.

Generally the morning is divided into five periods, and one of these is given to private study. The rule is to have one lesson in each subject studied *every day*, or, it may be, four days a week. This we consider one of the best features of the American High School system, and one most worthy of imitation. As the form system does not prevail, and as the various courses of study have to be fitted together in the time-table, the system somewhat resembles that of University College, London, or any similar institution. At a given hour a certain number of lessons are going on, attended by the pupils whose courses of study include those subjects; the others sit in special study halls, each at his or her own desk, or in the school library, doing private work. It should be noticed here that many of the pupils are only 15 years of age, and that they study in as orderly a manner as the older ones. At the close of a lesson period electric bells sound all over the building, the lessons stop, and from three to five minutes are allowed for the change of classes. The teacher usually remains in the same room, and the pupils move about freely and without supervision. Conversation is allowed during the change. Again and again we saw this process carried on, always in an admirable way; the pupils went about their business quickly and in an orderly manner; we could never detect, even by close observation, any undue levity or waste of time, and the buzz of conversation was no annoyance. It should also be remembered that in some cases as many as 700 young people were moving about all over a large building

simultaneously. At the close of the prescribed three
or five minutes, the electric bells sounded again and
absolute silence and order instantly followed. It is
a general rule to send any pupil, who may be late to
a lesson, immediately to the principal, to get from
him a written excuse, if reasonable cause can be
given ; if not, he deals with the matter as a breach
of order.

At " recess " the whole building is free to the
pupils. In a mixed school the boys go to the
basement and the playground adjoining, while the
upper floors are reserved for the girls. The principal is in charge during this time ; he stands in the
centre of the buildings, generally on the staircase,
or walks about. The teachers all retire to the
teachers' room, eat their own lunch, and rest until
the bell sounds. The theory of this is that, as the
principal does not teach as many hours as the rest
of the staff, and as he has greater authority, he
should be on duty during " recess." In some schools
there is a lady Vice-Principal, and she is responsible
for the girls during the same interval. The girls
often dance during some part of this time. In one
school we saw them using the great assembly hall
for this purpose, but we did not meet with any case
of open-air games for them except in private schools.
We repeatedly questioned teachers as to whether
any difficulties arose from allowing so complete a
measure of freedom during recess, over a large
building, to several hundreds of girls, but they
unanimously declared—many of them after years of
experience—that no evil results followed. " We

trust our young people," they said, "and they become worthy of our trust."

At the close of the morning's work, we observed
in several schools an excellent custom of formal
dismissal. The boys and girls march out from their
class-rooms, separately, to music; the girls generally
dress in the cloak-rooms or "wardrobes" adjoining
the schoolroom, the boys march to the basement.
We also observed some admirable marching from
the assembly hall after prayers, and the most
careful observation of a teacher accustomed to such
work failed to detect any talking, or other symptom
of disorder, on such occasions.

The week consists of five days, Saturday being
a whole holiday. The school year is about forty
weeks long; the summer vacation begins in June,
and ends in the beginning of September; private
schools close early in June, and open about September 20th. There are two short vacations of
about a week at Christmas and Easter. When the
year is divided into terms, these are reckoned
irrespective of vacations. There are three public
holidays—Thanksgiving Day, some Thursday in
late autumn, appointed by the President of the
United States by proclamation; Washington's
birthday, February 22nd; and Memorial Day, May
30th, to commemorate the soldiers who fell in the
war of 1861–1865. In the school session before
these last two holidays, patriotic exercises are held
in many schools, as lessons in civic duties and privileges. It should be remarked that a teacher's duties
in the public schools cease with the morning session,

unless there is a teachers' meeting; the principal, however, and the staff of his office generally remain.

Parents who wish their girls to learn music make arrangements privately; no such lessons, except class singing, are given in connection with the public High Schools. Drawing is a regular school subject, generally optional, and is given with the other lessons in the morning. Needlework and cooking, if taught at all, belong to the lower school (the grammar school).

It would be contrary to the spirit of the American public school system to have backward pupils return in the afternoon for special teaching; the school is free, and therefore it would be considered unjust to give one pupil more teaching than another. Such special help, if necessary, must be provided by the parents.

The amount of time given to home lessons varies in different schools. For High School pupils, about three hours a day is probably the average; many teachers state that such is their expectation. Most schools arrange for at least one study period each morning *in school*. In the Cambridge High School, one lesson at least is to be learnt at home—probably two, but here two study hours are given in school each day, the period being from 8·30 to 1·30. Thus the time spent on preparation is more than three hours, but then much of it is taken during the school time. There is an excellent plan in the Boston Girls' High and Latin Schools; home lessons are not prepared for every class lesson, one or two lessons being given every day, for which there is nothing done out of class. The principal informed us that this plan was adopted to prevent over-work. In the High School, Ann Arbor, where the strain of preparing for the University of Michigan is felt somewhat severely, the students are considered fortunate if they get their work done in four hours. The rules of the Board of Education of the public schools of San Francisco require that the total time for home study shall not exceed three and a half hours daily; at least, one hour a day is there required to be set apart for study in school. An inquiry was recently held there as to whether the parents considered there was too much home work set; 59% replied in the affirmative, 41% were satisfied with the existing rule.

It was impossible for the writer to inquire as to whether there is over-work in American schools, and even if time had allowed of inquiry, it would have been difficult to obtain definite results; one point may be mentioned however,—the great consideration for the health and comfort of girls and of women teachers, shown by both principals and superintendents. Again and again, on explaining some English custom, we were told that it could not be adopted because it would involve too great a strain on the health of girls or teachers; this is one reason given for not having many examinations, and for making those they have of less importance than with us. Several principals complained of the injury to girls' studies and health, caused by social engagements, parties, Sunday-school work, and church work.

We have already alluded to the large sums devoted to school buildings in America, and to the consequent magnificence of many of these. A remarkable case which is often quoted is that of the city of Duluth, on Lake Superior, which has a population of 35,000. It has recently erected a High School building costing $300,000 (£60,000), with a tower and wings, and finished inside with polished hardwood.

As a rule, school buildings are entirely detached from other houses, standing in the centre of what is called a "lot," and often at the corner of two streets; there is thus ample provision for light and air. The floor space is generally much greater than that in English schools ; not only are separate desks the rule, but there is a broad passage-way all round the room between the desks and the wall, in all the newer buildings. The corridors and staircases are very wide, and this is perhaps one cause of the ease of movement of large numbers.

To an Englishwoman the ventilation is, in general, deficient, though much attention is supposed to be given to the subject, and many systems of artificial ventilation are used. Some schools, *e.g.*, the Cambridge English High School, are admirably ventilated. The heating is to English ideas excessive, the standard being 70°; the temperature, however, often rises above this. We cannot but attribute to this cause much of the pallor of girls and women teachers, and the languor of their movements. In one school in a large Eastern city, on a day early in April, the writer was obliged to go out into the open air at every interval between lessons, in consequence of the heat and closeness of the atmosphere. This was, however, a building of the older style, containing 1,700 pupils.

The schoolrooms are well furnished, the desks and chairs being of excellent types. We noticed a particularly good form of chair for such lessons as involve the use of a book. It resembled a Windsor arm-chair with a cane or wood seat, and a movable flap on the right arm sufficiently large to hold the note-book. These chairs are much used in the American college lecture halls, and in schoolrooms for small divisions, for which they are very convenient.

All schoolrooms are surrounded with blackboards fixed to the wall; they begin at a convenient height from the floor (twenty inches for little children), and are four to five feet high. It might be thought that this would make the room dark and dull, but such is not the case, for the rooms are well lit, and the wall space above the blackboard tinted in light colours, and often ornamented with pictures and busts. Besides this, the board itself is covered with drawings and written work. The appearance of the rooms is pleasant, and, to a visitor, the mass of written matter on the walls peculiarly interesting and suggestive; it must be even more useful to the pupils themselves, as they see a record of the whole lesson which appeals to the eye, and thus makes a deeper impression than is possible when old work has to be rubbed out to make way for the new. What is put on the blackboard is almost entirely the work of the pupils ; the amount of space makes it possible for the teacher to draw illustrations for her lessons at convenient times, and these illustrations remain till wanted,—sometimes for several days. We saw some admirable maps, diagrams, abstracts, and analyses, etc., the work both of teachers and pupils.

Frequently in a mathematical lesson ten or fifteen pupils would be working algebra or geometry at the board at one time ; this was done quickly and simply with quiet self-reliance. It formed a convenient method of ascertaining whether the pupils knew their work or not. The writer cannot speak too strongly of the value of this simple device of a continuous blackboard ; most English schools have much to learn from America in this respect. Dr. Fitch, in his *Notes on American Schools and Training Colleges*, highly recommends the American blackboard system.

In the Girls' Latin School at Baltimore, we saw blinds which pulled up from the bottom of the window, as well as ordinary blinds falling from the top ; thus the light could be exactly regulated.

It is difficult to give any general account of a typical High School building. We did not meet with any example of the English type of schoolrooms opening from a great hall, or of tiers of rooms opening into corridors, as in the City of London School for boys. The American type is a square building, three or four stories high, with a corridor in each story down the middle, and rooms opening from each side of it. There is often a second corridor crossing this at right angles, the staircase being near the intersection of the two corridors. At the corners of the building are large study halls, with windows in the two adjacent sides, and smaller rooms opening out on the inner sides to the corridors. Each of these large halls is devoted to one class (*i.e.*, year), every pupil having a separate desk there. These halls are occasionally used for lessons, but the system of having several different lessons going on simultaneously in a large hall, with or without curtains, seems absolutely unknown in American High Schools, whether public or private.

We did not see a proper gymnasium in any public school; there is generally a room in the basement devoted to physical exercises, but it is often low, dark, and dull-looking.

At the top of the square block of building is the assembly hall, used for prayers and other formal meetings of the whole school. This hall is often large, but seldom lofty, and lacks the beauty and dignity of our well-known school halls. The Normal College, New York, and the Girls' High School, Brooklyn, which each contain nearly 2,000 pupils, have separate lofty halls, adjoining the schoolrooms, which resemble an English concert hall, but except for size they are not impressive. The assembly hall of the Girls' High School, Boston, is however so exquisitely and suitably decorated that the writer feels obliged to describe it in full.

When the school house was built in 1870, some members of the American Social Science Association offered to contribute and place in the hall various casts from antique sculpture and statuary, if the city would fit up the hall to receive them. This was done. The walls of the hall (62 feet square) are divided by Doric pilasters into panels, painted a soft neutral tint. These form the background for various statues or busts. Above an architrave has been constructed for a series of slabs from the Parthenon. There are ten statues and eleven busts: they include the Venus of Milo, the Diana of Gabii, and the Polyhymnia from the Louvre; the Pudicitia and Demosthenes of the Vatican, and busts of Jupiter, Pericles, and the Young Augustus from the same gallery, and other famous works. It is impossible to imagine any more beautiful or suitable decoration for a school hall: its austere beauty must needs have an ethical influence on the pupils. The principal of the school occasionally after prayers gives a short address to the girls to lead them to appreciate these masterpieces of art.

In two other schools we saw casts of the Parthenon Frieze used as decoration for a large room: one was in the Bryn Mawr School at Baltimore (private), the other the Lincoln School at Brookline, Mass. (public elementary). In the latter case it was the gift of a citizen to a school attended chiefly by the poorest children of the district, in order that they might have the highest ideal of beauty placed before them in their school lives.

Further details on school houses and fittings are to be found in the Bureau of Education Circular, "City School Systems in the United States."

The discipline of American schools, both elementary and secondary, cannot be too highly approved. It is the more admirable as it seems to be entirely a matter for the pupils. There are very few rules, no system of small punishments, no elaborate supervision by teachers; the young people govern themselves. As before stated, we again and again watched for such small breaches of order as habitually occur even in good schools in England, but none were noticed. The degree of attention in class was occasionally inadequate, but the pupils always seemed to know their work, and were probably attending, even while seeming not to do so. During the whole time of our visiting schools, we never heard a teacher reprove a pupil for disorder. Dr. Harris, in his Report on the Public School of the District of Columbia (*i.e.*, Washington), states that he " went into 300 rooms, and never once heard a teacher reprove a pupil for disorder." Much more might be said on this point; it is enough to repeat that the discipline is excellent.

The writer repeatedly questioned American teachers as to how this admirable result was secured. They attributed it first of all to the national character, and second to the system of trusting the pupils. Mr. Bryce alludes to the optimism which is so marked a feature of American social life; it is none the less prominent in the schools. We subjoin an extract expressing American opinion, from the Calendar (Prospectus) of the Cambridge High School :—

" It is presumed that pupils in this school mean to conduct themselves honourably and becomingly, a presumption justified by the commendable behaviour of nearly all. It is the aim of the school to strengthen the sense of propriety, duty, and honour by trusting it. Boys and girls at school are *citizens* as fully as they can ever be (see Sect. I., Art. XIV., Const. U.S.); it becomes them, therefore, in school and elsewhere now, as throughout their lives, to practise the duties, cultivate the graces, and display the loyalty of good American citizenship. Only in cases of conspicuous failure in conduct will a deportment record be kept." The head master states officially, "I am convinced that any system of discipline which does not strengthen the self-directive faculties is unsatisfactory. Self-control is the ultimate object of all training, physical and intellectual as well as moral, This is to be attained not by a policy of repression, but by granting a large degree of liberty. Artificial standards, unnatural restrictions, are unwise, because they do not prepare for what comes after school. They unnecessarily irritate the pupil, and in the end do him no good. Sternness and severity are not so much needed as firmness tempered by kindness, and a prompt recognition of every honest effort to correct a fault."

The present Superintendent of Philadelphia informed the writer that discipline has been softened and improved by *women's* teaching: it was once harsh and severe. Other authorities state that a more military and rigid system prevailed till a few years ago. This strict system tended, it is said, " to sap vitality and prevent pupils from working for themselves."

The Superintendent of Brookline, Mass., who has had a wide experience in other cities, states in his last Report :—

"Still another gratifying tendency is the attempt to apply in school-management the theory of self-government, to do away as much as possible with the necessity for authority and repression. An appeal is made to the highest motives, such as honour, manly pride and courtesy, until these are incorporate in the school. This idea that a school should train the young for their social duties in a free republic is not new. Hosts of teachers are applying this principle and are working toward high ideals of character. Schools thus conducted constitute the only safeguard of a nation where there is the largest degree of individual freedom consistent with the common good."

One teacher of experience said to the writer, " Young America takes school seriously, and goes to school as to business." It should be remembered that the young people in the High School have gone through eight years' regular training in the elementary school, where the discipline is more strict, though equally kindly.

The fact that the public High School is *free* also tends to make attendance a privilege. If the pupils are not prepared to conduct themselves properly in school, they are warned that expulsion will follow. Although the number of cases of expulsion is, as far as we could learn, comparatively small, we believe it is larger than in England, where it is only used in very exceptional cases. The rules about attendance are in America extremely strict : Pupils who do not attend the public schools regularly are dismissed ; this is the easier, as, in most cities, the number applying for admission to the High Schools is in excess of the accommodation. In one case, Ann Arbor, absence for two days without due cause (to be late counts as half one absence), in four weeks, means dismissal from the school. It is probable that the rigorous rules as to attendance exclude from the school those who are not in earnest, and thus help to keep up the standard of discipline and efficiency. The private schools seem able to be much more rigorous than might be expected, in consequence of the high standard set by the public schools. They generally require parents to pay the fees for a whole year on the entry of a pupil; they, with other educational institutions, demand " certificates of honourable dismissal " from pupils who come to them from other schools. They seem also indifferent to the withdrawal of girls who cannot or will not keep up with the class. The principal of one private school in Baltimore which prepares for College, informed the writer that seventeen pupils had withdrawn between September and April, because they found the Latin too difficult. It is, of course, impossible for a stranger to judge of this matter fully in a few weeks of observation; the above remarks are only put forward tentatively. Difference of national characteristics and of public sentiment affect school discipline very largely. We were informed by the Professor of Ethics at one of the great American Universities, that it was an American principle to leave the individual perfect freedom of choice, and that this was the only way to train young people to true morality and self-control. Even if, under this system, some of the weaker members succumbed to temptation, it is considered better to allow this to happen than to restrain all, and thus make it impossible for them ever to learn true self-government.

In accordance with these ethical principles, the system of prizes is banished; there are in some schools

a few special prizes, but there is nothing corresponding to the system prevalent in many English schools.
Marks are used to some extent in most schools, but
the best authorities seem to disapprove of what
they term the percentage system, *i.e.*, the estimating
a scholar's position by the percentage of marks
obtained. They prefer a scale of credits by letters
(A = very good, B = good, and so on), similar to that
used in the detailed individual reports of our Cambridge Local Examinations. Again and again we
found a superintendent expressing this view in his
report. Dr. Brooks, of Philadelphia, says, " to train
a pupil to recite for a recitation mark, is to give
him an absolutely wrong idea of education, and
tends to destroy his taste for study and knowledge."
The superintendent of Ann Arbor says, " I believe
no pedagogical principle is better established than
that the most fruitful motive of a student's efforts is
internal—not external—interest in the subject matter of study, rather than the teacher's will, honour
prizes, or high per-cents. The normal condition of
mind growth is freedom—voluntary activity. More-
over, the good teacher will do her best work under
conditions of freedom—freedom as to methods,
quantity of subject matter presented in a given
time, form of pupils' acquisitions, and all the details
of inciting and impressing her pupils. I trust we
are for ever done with the repressing influences of
the examination for promotion. . . . I deem
it worthy of mention here that the High School (as
well as most of lower grades) has abandoned the
percentage method of recording standings, using

F

instead only four grades of scholarship, denoted by letters. We have long observed that many pupils are accustomed to rate themselves by their percentage record, rather than by their conscious power and attainment. We believe that artificial incentives of any kind are likely to break down the ethical spirit in youth which is the chief element in genuine character and high attainment. Scholarship honours in some degree seem inevitable in school management, but they should never be regarded by pupil or teacher as the highest motive of study."

The teacher's estimate is considered by some authorities the best criterion of a pupil's progress. "The examination paper still attacks learning on its intellectual side, the marking system on its moral." [1] Some schools send home monthly reports to the parents in a book, keeping a counterfoil in their own register; the Cambridge High and Latin Schools, and the Brearly School, New York, have excellent forms for this purpose,—concise, simple, and clear.

There is a very strong feeling against examinations among American educators. The principal of an excellent High School told the writer that he considered them the " bane of teaching "; the superintendent of Philadelphia, in his last annual report, strongly deprecates any encouragement of the examination system. The superintendent of Cambridge (Mass.), takes the same view. "After an added experience of ten years, I would state

---

[1] G. N. Palmer in *Andover Review*, Nov. 1885.

positively that I do not believe in written examinations, the results of which are to determine, or to be a factor in determining, the fitness of pupils for promotion. These examinations set up a low and alluring end for study—the attainment of examination marks—and they dissipate that natural desire for knowledge, which is the source and inspiration of all true learning and of all real joy in study." [1]

Even promotion examinations given by the teachers themselves, or by the superintendent, are considered injurious by many of the most eminent authorities.[2] Thus the public High Schools do not send in their pupils for University examinations such as the Harvard examination. Although this is an excellent examination, only 69 girls, nearly all from private schools, have passed it since 1881. Its syllabus, we may add, somewhat resembles that of the Matriculation Examination of the University of London, but it is probably not quite so difficult, as it can be taken in two parts.

The public High Schools prepare for College to some extent: this means that their students have to pass a matriculation examination somewhat below the standard of the Harvard examinations. Even in this matter, however, the feeling is so strongly against examinations, that many Colleges admit,

---

[1] This speech is quoted by the Cambridge superintendent from Dr. White, *Cam. School Report.*

[2] *Boston Report,* pp. 18, 19, 25, 26. *Washington Report,* p. 34. *Forum,* Dr. Rice (March, 1893): "Regular examinations for promotions are now looked upon as unscientific pedagogy."

"on certificate," as it is termed, from good schools.
This system originated, we believe, in the University of Michigan : we give some account of it in
Chapter VI. It means that a College recognises, as
an exemption, a certificate from the principal of a
good school that his pupil has satisfactorily gone
through a certain course, including the subjects
required for matriculation.

There is a very strong divergence of opinion on
this point among American educators ; those who
approve of it consider that the teacher, after knowing and working with a pupil for years, is a better
judge of his fitness for College than an examiner
who has read a few papers. On the other hand, so
great an authority as President Eliot, of Harvard,
considers the certificate system essentially bad.

" The method of admission on certificate which
has grown out of this relation between State
Universities and secondary schools is so full of perils
both for the schools and the university, that
Harvard University has no desire to enter on any
such policy." [1] Harvard refuses to admit "on
certificate," and so does Bryn Mawr, one of the most
distinguished of the women's Colleges.

As we have noticed in Chapter I., in speaking of
the High School Board of Minnesota, and the
Regents of the University of the State of New
York, there is a tendency to introduce examinations
in the State system, as a means of securing

---

[1] *Annual Report of the President to Treasurer of Harvard
University*, 1891-1892.

efficiency, and of raising the standard of attainment.

Every properly fitted school in America possesses an excellent library, which is largely used by the pupils. There seems usually to be a librarian on the staff, who is expected to help the students to use the books, during the study hours before alluded to, and at home. As is explained in the Chapter on Method, pupils are expected to get up subjects for themselves ; this they do in great part through the school library. The *Encyclopædia Britannica* and the *Century Dictionary* are found in many such libraries ; that of Washington, containing 5,600 vols., is open to pupils from 2 to 3.30 each day, under charge of the librarian. At the Ann Arbor High School, Michigan, the library consists of 4,480 vols., and is supplied with the best magazines and periodicals. " The library is made an important adjunct to the school in its regular work, especially in studies in history, the sciences, and literature. An experienced librarian is in attendance to furnish pupils with books, or to guide them in the work of research." We frequently entered these school libraries, and found the students working there very much as readers do in the British Museum. The risk of injury or loss does not seem to be so much considered, if only a number of pupils can be induced to use the books. The report of the Cambridge High School, which has a very fine library, states : " The books are easily accessible, for closed cases have been abandoned, and pains taken to make their use inviting and easy. It is better to let books get mixed a little, or even to risk an occasional loss, than to set guard on them so that it becomes hard, if not disagreeable, to get at them."

In the great University Library at Harvard, there is an excellent plan which might be adopted in schools possessing a library. The professors each draw up a list of books useful in the courses they are giving ; the librarian selects these from the library and places them together, each set on separate shelves, in an alcove round a table, the name of the course and the professor being placed on the alcove. The students can go and work at the tables, using the books as they please during the day, and can take any books home between 5 p.m. and 9 a.m. next morning. The writer saw this arrangement in working order, and was much impressed by its usefulness. By such means students can be trained to use a library who would otherwise never learn to depend on themselves.

We do not propose to enter into any details regarding the number of pupils in a given school. Local conditions govern this matter : a small town will have a small High School, a large city may have one great school with 2,000 girls, as in New York or Philadelphia, or may have several High Schools in different parts of the city, as Boston does. There the 3,488 pupils are distributed among ten schools. The public schools have usually larger numbers than ours, and the classes are larger. Boston even has an average of 31·3 girls to a teacher in the Latin School, and 34·0 in the English High School. This will seem to English teachers too large for thoroughness, especially in teaching such subjects as Latin and mathematics. Probably one reason why the private schools do so much of the work of preparing for College is that the classes in them are smaller.

The idea of economy is probably the reason for the existence of such great city schools as those of New York and Philadelphia. "A mammoth school," says one authority, " can never be a good school." Whether this be so or not, it certainly seems to the writer that the very large schools in America are inferior to the smaller, particularly in that spirit of freedom, and that happiness and self-activity, which is the especial merit of American schools. The High School of Brooklyn, with its fine staff of teachers, is a marvel of organization. But even there, as it seemed to us, something was lost by the necessity of excessive attention to those details of discipline necessary when dealing with 1,800 girls under one roof. It may be a mere coincidence, but the most ideal schools we visited were those whose numbers were comparatively low.

In some cities the Girl's High School is also a normal school, girls taking the High School course, with a few lessons in pedagogy as a preparation for the work of teaching in the public schools. This system is gradually becoming obsolete, and the best authorities do not approve of it, a separate and normal school with a purely professional course being preferred. However, a very large number of girls in a public High School look forward to teaching in the elementary schools of the city; probably this is one reason of the large numbers seeking admission.

CHAPTER III.

ON this subject it is very difficult to make any general statements; such schools naturally differ much more *inter se* than the public schools. Their special function is, according to high educational authority, to make experiments, to explore new paths in education, or rather, to vary the metaphor, to act as a nursery ground in which variations which naturally arise may be cultivated and tested, thence to be transplanted to the regular gardens of the public schools.

A particularly interesting example of this function is a private school for girls in New York. Here the principles of Herbart and Rein, his disciple, are being put into practice; the whole curriculum is arranged according to the " concentration " theory, and the lessons are illustrated by excellent sets of diagrams. The organization of the school deserves careful study, but it does not seem possible to give a clear account in writing. The system must be seen to be appreciated. One peculiarity is that the staff is largely male, the chief posts being held by men of high University rank.

Private schools may be divided into two classes. The first consists of *Elementary* schools, founded by various religious bodies, especially the Roman Catholic Church, and known as parochial schools. These present features of special interest, but are outside the scope of the present inquiry. The second class are the private secondary schools, corresponding to those in England ; Americans, however, include in this category such schools as are not conducted for private profit, but are governed by a Board. Thus our girls' Endowed and Proprietary schools, which we term public, would be called private in America. There are, however, comparatively few such *schools*, though there are many so-called *colleges* giving really only a secondary education, whose legal status is very similar to that of an English Endowed School, only that in America there is no Charity Commission or other central body to control endowed educational institutions.

In New England there are certain schools termed Academies which prepare largely for College : these are comparatively ancient ; they have endowments and trustees. Time did not permit a visit to any of these ; they appear, however, to be more important for boys than girls. There is a strong tendency in the Eastern cities to establish schools similar to our High Schools for girls, and we visited two of these, one in Baltimore and one in New York. In Philadelphia the Society of Friends has for many years past maintained High Schools both for boys and girls. The reason for this tendency, as given by Americans themselves, is the injurious influence on the public school system of the corrupt municipal life of the great Eastern cities, with their mobs of ignorant foreign immigrants. Details of this disease

can be found in Bryce's "American Commonwealth."
Reference to this[1] will show that such conditions must
affect the public schools of these cities, however earnest the superintendents and teachers may be.   The
series of articles in *The Forum*, by Dr. Rice, also
illustrates this point.

The writer paid particular attention to a school in
New York, which appears to be in the transition
state between a school conducted for private profit,
and what in England would be a regular Endowed
High School.   Its pupils are drawn in great part
from the highest circles of New York society, and its
fees are correspondingly large, amounting to $350
(£70).   This sum allows for a large staff, 24 to 200
pupils.   It is governed by a Board of Directors, two
of whom are women, the Chairman being the pastor
of a leading church in New York.

It is difficult to furnish any statistics as to the
proportion of girls and boys receiving secondary
education in private schools, as compared with those
attending the free public day schools.   In Massachusetts 10.6% of the children are in parochial schools,
and 2.4% in other private schools.   The Bureau of
Education Report for 1889–90 states that one-eighth
of the pupils are in private schools; in older and
wealthier sections one-sixth ; in others in some cases
one-thirteenth.   We subjoin in the Appendix a detailed statement from the same report as to pupils
receiving secondary education in private schools.

Experienced American educators say that private

---

[1] Vol. ii. Part iii. (passim).   Vol. i., Chaps. L., LI., LII.

secondary schools are more numerous and important in the East and are comparatively unimportant (in some districts indeed entirely unknown) in the West.[1] They also state that the rise of social distinctions has much to do with the development of private secondary schools, especially for girls. Other reasons of more weight from a pedagogic point of view are given for their success and popularity ; these are, that the payment of fees, often very large fees,[2] allows of a more expensive staff, and of smaller classes, and consequent greater attention to individuals. The good private schools employ a very large proportion of distinguished College graduates, including men and women who have taken high honours at the English Universities. It was the writer's experience, of course a somewhat limited one, to hear very much better teaching in private schools than in public schools, except in New England.

Preparation for College is largely the work of private schools, possibly because they can give more attention to individuals. We were informed by persons competent to give an opinion, that in New England and the West there is a closer connection between the public High Schools and the Colleges, than elsewhere. The writer visited five high-class boarding schools, which resembled women's colleges in their social life, in their atmosphere of culture and refinement, and in the freedom of their discipline. We

---

[1] There is not a single private secondary school in Ann Arbor, Michigan, a town of 8,000 inhabitants.

[2] £20-£70 for tuition ; £100-£200 for boarding.

also heard excellent teaching given in the schools, and formed a very favourable opinion of them, so far as a short visit could enable a stranger to judge. It is usual to have a separate staff of ladies, often of mature age and great social experience, to conduct any supervision that may be necessary out of school hours, the strain of teaching being considered enough for the ordinary teachers. At one school we visited there is a special system of boarding houses separate from the school, the founder considering that it is injurious to growing girls to be in the same atmosphere and to deal with the same persons during school, and out of school.

We visited one of the houses for the girls attending this school. It is a charmingly appointed building, arranged for ten or twelve girls, and headed by a House Mother, a lady of culture and social gifts, who makes a real home for the girls, the rules being only those of a well regulated family. This arrangement is valued for its refining and softening influence on the character of the pupils; they are dealt with individually rather than in the aggregate, and thus there is no need of the " military discipline " and the " incomprehensible rules which go far to blunt the child's finer nature."

There is apparently not so much difference between the curriculum in private and public schools as might be expected. Perhaps there is a tendency to do less science, and more history and literature, in private schools. In both, Latin and mathematics are studied.

CHAPTER IV.

METHOD.

THE method of actual teaching in American schools differs much from that in use in England. It centres in the text-book, at least for general High School work. For younger children the oral method is naturally the one employed; German influence in pedagogics has also done much in the elementary schools. But the young men and women of the High School are not children, to whom things have to be explained; the ideal for them is to teach them how to get knowledge for themselves. Nothing strikes an English teacher more forcibly on first listening to lessons in American schools, than the important place the text-book takes. Indeed the word "lesson" is rarely used; "recitation" is the phrase. This implies what is generally the case, that the period is to be devoted by the pupils to the recital of what they have learnt by their own study from the book. American educationalists claim that there is in this a special advantage; namely, that the varied minds of the pupils, each apprehending the subject in a different way, and each contributing his share to the common recitation, give a greater width and interest to the work than if, as in the oral method, the teacher's personality were the only one active. If the teacher gives the information orally, the class can only follow the subject from her point of view ; and her way of thinking, it is said, is imposed on the mind of the pupil.

New work is not, as a rule, gone over in the class first ; the pupil makes acquaintance with fresh knowledge by struggling with its difficulties alone. The cleverer pupils overcome these ; at the lesson they recite for the benefit of their duller companions and for their own. The teacher questions the class, and it is supposed that all difficulties are thus cleared up, and that, by some additional private study, even the slowest will understand the whole matter.

In all the lessons heard by the writer the questioning was, without exception, good, whether its object was to bring out the knowledge self-acquired by the pupil, or to clear up difficulties. We did not, however, hear much of the pedagogic exercise known as eliciting a point.

This recitation method may seem to some to run counter to educational theory, and such persons would doubtless at once condemn it. It certainly has its faults; chief among these is *dulness*. Of course, in the hands of an especially clever teacher, it may be made lively, and may, as its supporters argue, bring the pupils' minds to converge on the subject and illustrate it from various points of view. But in general, these recitations seem to an English teacher to lack animation and interest, and she is surprised to find how attentive the students appear to be. There is also danger that the more backward and feeble pupils may never really understand the subject at all,[1] for the teacher does not as a rule explain difficulties, as an English teacher does, so that even the dullest may understand. The tendency towards excessive use of the memory is so obvious as to need no comment.[2]

But for all this the recitation method deserves the careful study of English teachers—at all events, in girls' High Schools, where too often, as a satirist remarked, "the teacher learns the lessons and says them to the girls." Its great merit is that it makes the pupil self-dependent and teaches him to work for himself, *to learn how to read*, and to acquire knowledge by reading. Such is one great aim of American education. Unless a pupil, on leaving the High School, knows how to study alone, the teacher thinks his work is a failure, however much enthusiasm or information a pupil may have.

The success of the method is aided in America by several conditions, as yet rare in England. First, the text-books there are much better than ours. This is due to one important fact: there is more money spent on them, not only more absolutely,— for prices are generally higher in the New World,— but more relatively. Many districts supply text-books free ; Massachusetts does, and is well satisfied with the system, which seems to be spreading. But even when the parents are required to buy books,

---

[1] See *Teaching of Mathematics, infra*, pp. 85–88.
[2] Examples of the Recitation Method are to be found in *Methods and Aids in Geography* (C. F. King), p. 207, where a large paragraph recounts the many books used by the pupils.

they do so far more willingly than in England, not only because they do not in the public schools pay for schooling, but because the habit of buying books is much more a national custom there than here.

Often an English teacher cannot make her pupils depend on themselves for getting up the subject, because the only text-book that can be afforded is meagre or even obsolete, and she is the only person who has access to a really good book.

Another favourable condition is the study hour in school every day, which seems to be the general custom. Out of the five periods into which the school day is divided, one at least is devoted to private study, the pupils sitting in the large halls or the school library. They can there use the works of reference with which every good school is provided, or may receive hints from a teacher. This excellent custom is of course only possible when few subjects are studied. In addition to the good school libraries, the local public library is often drawn upon by special arrangement. Indeed, in the practical use of libraries, English people have much to learn from America. Another point is the absence of external examinations, with their independent standard. If the teacher prepares a subject carefully for the mental digestion of a pupil, and gives it in the form in which it can be most easily assimilated, she is clearly more likely to have her pupils pass examinations than if she made them do all the work themselves, especially if the preparation for the examination is short. The weak ones, too, can thus be helped to pass.

The American method is better suited to the stronger members of a class; it fits them for life rather than for examinations. We were much impressed with the development of self-reliance visible even at a cursory glance in American schools. In one room, young people may be studying, without any supervision, in perfect order and in a business-like manner; or they are moving about quietly to fetch books or reference dictionaries.

In a class lesson, they take notes as they like of a new point mentioned by the teacher or a fellow pupil; they are ready when asked to recite from their own store of information. They are often required to keep their own notes without any revision of note-books by the teacher; the responsibility comes on them.

We did not notice a single case of the phenomenon so common in English schools, when a pupil has given up all effort to understand, and throws herself entirely on the teacher for an explanation. The writer frequently asked principals and other teachers of experience how this general habit of self-reliance was acquired. They connected it with the political institutions and religious and social ideals of the country; but it was so natural to them that they were unable to throw any further light on the subject.

The Teaching of Mathematics.

In American schools arithmetic is included under the title Mathematics; but as it is not, properly speaking, a High School subject, the writer did not devote particular attention to the methods of teach-

G

ing it.   Number is begun in the primary classes, and it occupies a large proportion of the pupils' time between 9 and 15 years of age.   American educators are at the present time vigorously discussing whether this share is not excessive, and what subjects should be introduced instead.

In some places arithmetic is taught in the first year of the High School course; in others, which prepare for College, the demands of the entrance examination in arithmetic require that some part of the last year only should be given to revision; apparently, it is not otherwise included in the curriculum at all.

The exclusion of arithmetic before mentioned leaves much time to be given to the study of mathematics proper, a lesson often being given every day. It is the almost universal custom to study algebra before geometry; [1] two reasons are given for this: first, that it follows naturally on the study of arithmetic, and second, that geometry is made very much easier by the adoption of algebraic methods.   In some cities (notably in Brooklyn, New York, and Washington, District of Columbia) the elements of algebra are taught in the last year of the grammar school course.   By the kindness of the superintendent of Brooklyn, we had the opportunity of inspecting their examination papers, and were much impressed by the neatness and accuracy of the work and the high average standard of attainment.

---

[1] Bureau of Education Circular on the Teaching of Mathematics.

In general, however, algebra is not studied at all till the first year of the High School, when the pupils, who begin the subject in September, have worked through Quadratics by the following June, having four or five lessons a week. Some High Schools go further in the year, though the subject is usually finished in the second year. In the lessons we heard, the pupils seemed to be very intelligent and to thoroughly understand their work, a large proportion of the class being engaged in working out problems on the blackboard round the room. In every case in which the home-work was examined, it was found to have been done in pencil on rough scribbling paper; but the methods were correct and the work was accurate, while the number of problems worked voluntarily showed the interest taken in the subject.

We had no means of ascertaining whether the fundamental principles of algebra, and the more abstract parts of the subject were as thoroughly mastered. Such examination papers as we saw contained few, if any, really difficult examples. We think, however, that the general average in good schools is higher than in the corresponding schools in England; that is, there is a larger percentage of girls doing elementary algebra of a given degree of difficulty there than with us, though few, in American High Schools proper, would reach the standard of the Senior Cambridge Local Examination.

The text-books were in general excellent, and would enable an intelligent boy or girl to master

the easy parts of the subject without any aid whatever from a teacher.

In algebra generally, adoption of the text-book
method, in the lessons we heard, was very marked ;
the pupils did all the work, the teacher's duty being
to direct their energies and to ask questions, in order
to have difficulties explained by the more intelligent
members of the class.

Many schools sent excellent work in algebra, to
the World's Fair ; we admired especially the papers
from schools in Massachusetts, California, and Minnesota.

The course of study in geometry differs largely
from that current in England, the Euclidian system
being generally abandoned. To understand the
American method, it is necessary to read one of the
books employed, the most popular being Wentworth's, which apparently is thorough and well
arranged. It treats of the straight line and the
circle first, then of proportional lines and similar
polygons, going on to areas of polygons and the
properties of regular polygons and circles. The
latter part is devoted to solid geometry, the subjects
of Euclid XI., and the properties of polyhedrons, the
cylinder, cone, and sphere.

This course is generally covered in a year, the less
ambitious schools not attempting solid geometry,
which, in America, is a College subject. As in
algebra, four or five lessons per week are given. Some
of the more progressive schools are introducing, into
the early years of the High School course or the
latter years of the grammar school, a series of

lessons in form, practical geometry, etc., termed in the Boston Latin School, "Objective Geometry," which is intended as a preparation for the more rigid and logical study of later years. The text-book most in favour for this part of the work is Spencer's "Inventional Geometry." We heard an excellent lesson, based on this work, given to a class of backward girls in a good private school in Philadelphia. This book, written by the father of Herbert Spencer, has, unfortunately, long been out of print, but it is now, we believe, reprinted in England, and is well worth the attention of English teachers.

No subject has seemed to us more difficult, or has involved more thought and inquiry than this question of the teaching of geometry. To make any definite report upon it is almost impossible, the differences between American and English education being more marked here than anywhere. One positive statement can be made : the actual properties of figures, the formulæ for areas, etc., are more carefully studied than with us, and seem to be thoroughly well known. This is brought out clearly by the answers to that questioning which is apparently the most important part of the mathematical teacher's duty. If the object of the study of geometry in schools is to fit young people to be engineers, architects, surveyors, designers, etc., then this system is admirable. To estimate the degree of logical training gained by the average boy or girl is a much more delicate matter. The usual method of a lesson is as follows :—

Certain pages of the text-book having been set by the teacher, to be studied at home, she calls out about one-third of the class to draw figures on the board, and in turn to demonstrate the proofs of the propositions. The less intelligent pupils have then an opportunity of asking questions, which are generally answered by other members of the class. The teacher merely guides the work. After this some riders may be worked in the same way, the teacher first questioning the clever students, the others listening and understanding as well as they can. The questions from the teachers are as a rule excellent, but there seems to be little of that building up of the new work on the foundation of the old, by the simultaneous activity of teacher and class, that is the ideal of English mathematical teaching in schools.

This ideal was, however, seen in actual practice in the Brooklyn High School for Girls, and the Cambridge High School. In the latter we saw, also, excellent sets of solutions to riders, well arranged and neat. We saw similar sets in the Brearley School, New York. Riders involving numerical calculation, and the drawing of exact and careful figures, occur much more commonly than with us. The effect of this is to make geometry examination papers there much easier than, as a rule, they are in England. The percentage of marks required for a pass is also much higher in America.

The Boston High School for Girls uses no textbook. The girls listen to the demonstrations worked as riders by the more advanced members of the class, make their own notes, and are tested by the teacher's examination, written at stated periods, on which their promotion depends.   In general, the written work is much less than that done in England; "recitation" takes its place. The work sent by schools in California and Minnesota to the Chicago Exhibition appeared to be much above the average.

By the courtesy of the authorities of two schools we were allowed to give short lessons in geometry to two classes, and were much impressed by the general brightness and intelligence shown by the pupils in solving simple riders.   Much of this is, doubtless, due to the recitation method ; but we cannot help suspecting there is (as teachers who know both countries say) some psychological difference between the American and English student of mathematics.   To discuss this is, however, beyond the scope of the present inquiry.

Higher subjects are rarely studied in High Schools; some do a little *Trigonometry.*   Advanced schools often take *Solid Geometry* (properties and mensuration of solids, etc.).   We did not find any cases of the teaching of *Mechanics* as a mathematical subject; no great examination demands it, as does the Matriculation Examination of the University of London. *Astronomy* is studied much more generally than with us, but from a text-book as an information subject.

There seems to be nothing corresponding to the work done in our best schools by a few girls or boys in the sixth form, for scholarship examinations at the Universities.   Indeed the public school system would hardly allow of such special attention being given to a few. In private schools small classes are the rule, and the work thus seemed more thorough to an English spectator. We heard a good deal of the unpopularity of mathematics among pupils. Some principals considered that girls were conspicuously weaker in that subject than boys. At the same time, the subject is one held in respect by laymen, and considered a part of a liberal education for both sexes, even by persons of comparatively little culture. We were informed, for instance, that a local Board was generally willing to pay for a special mathematical teacher. It is often taught in private boarding schools, and is, we believe, always required for admission to College. Classics does not secure this general recognition, perhaps because of its less practical character.

Where there is so much popular feeling for the study of mathematics, and so much intelligence on the part of the pupils, it is strange that the subject should not raise more enthusiasm among American girls. We cannot but think that, in this subject, study of English methods of teaching might be of advantage to American teachers.

The Teaching of History.

This subject receives much more attention in American schools than in our own. Indeed, this statement holds good for the Universities also, where historical studies claim the devotion of a large number of the ablest undergraduates, and where, as in Johns Hopkins University, the number of graduates in the history and economics departments far exceeds that in any other.

To a visitor familiar with English Universities, where classics and mathematics count for so much, nothing in American College education is so remarkable, as the relative predominance of historical studies. Even in such an institution as the Mass. Institute of Technology, where the classics are excluded, and languages hold a subordinate place, the history department is one of the most vigorous, and some study of history is required of all students in the early years of the general course. The causes of this predominance are perhaps to be found in the existence of a written constitution which directs men's minds to the study of civics. Be this as it may, history is of far higher account in American schools than in ours. As the vast majority of the population never receive any higher education than that of the grammar school, it is necessary in a democratic country to give some instruction in the elements of political science, and in the national history, to the scholars in the common schools.

The amount of work differs, of course, in different schools, but the general programme is, to begin with, simple stories of great men, going on to outlines of United States history, and finishing, in the last year, with a study of the more abstract parts of the national history, such as the distinctions between parties, free trade and protection, etc., etc. We heard several lessons on such subjects, notably one in the Franklin School, Washington, where boys and girls of 14 to 15 showed considerable

intelligence in answering questions, and reciting
from their text-book, on political parties, the tariff
question, and State banks.

We read some examination papers, selected at
random from those written by boys and girls in the
grammar schools of Brooklyn, New York, for graduation at 15 years of age.   The subject was entitled,
" Civil Government."   The papers dealt with the
United States Senate, direct taxation, patent laws,
grand and petit juries, defined tribunal, felony,
insurrection, invasion, original and appelate jurisdiction, and quoted passages from the constitution.
The answers were well expressed, clear, and intelligent; and the per centage of marks gained was
high.

At the Chicago Exhibition there was a great deal
of excellent work shown in history, maps and
diagrams especially.   The Nebraska Exhibit sent
sets of maps, made by pupils, to show the growth
of the United States territorially, one superposed on
the others.   Oakland, California, showed diagrams
to illustrate the three divisions of the Federal
Government. In the High School English history is
studied, sometimes as a separate subject, sometimes
in its proper place in a course of general history.
Nearly every High School takes its pupils through
such a course, beginning with Egypt and Assyria,
going on to the classical period, and to mediæval
and modern times. There are several excellent text-
books in use, which deal rather with general
principles, the history of civilization, development
of thought, etc., than with masses of minute detail,

as is sometimes the case with the *Weltgeschichte* in German schools.

In the last year at the High School, the pupils study civics, that is, constitutional history and such elements of constitutional law, methods of government, etc., as are necessary for the intelligent performance of the duties of a citizen; this corresponds with the United States history taken in the last year of the grammar school, being directed to the same end, but more comprehensive in its character.

American educators feel very strongly the importance of this subject, as a preparation for citizenship.[1] Dr. McAlister, late Superintendent of Philadelphia, calls it, "a branch of study which is certainly second to no other in importance in the education of American children." This passage occurs in a syllabus prepared by him for the public schools of Philadelphia for children from 11 to 15 years of age.

The purpose of this instruction is there declared to be, "to inspire the young with a broad, sound, generous patriotism, and to train them for the right discharge, in due time, of the duties of citizenship." "The pupils should be made to see the evolution of the political institutions of the United States, in the progress of events from the planting of the Colonies to the present time, and to find in these political institutions the source of the freedom, stability, and power of the nation."

An example of the methods used to bring home to

---

[1] Buisson says on page 316 of his report that patriotism is as the national religion of America. "C'est là comme la religion nationale de l'Amérique."

the pupils the nature of their national institutions is a class exercise in civil government, given by the pupils of the English High School, Cambridge, Mass., at their graduating class (Speech Day), June 18th, 1890. In New England the old Teutonic Tungemot is still preserved, and local government is carried on by the citizens assembled in town meeting. The pupils, as a regular school exercise, had held a town meeting to discuss "whether towns and cities should provide flags for public school houses." This was reproduced by 27 pupils taking part, 16 being girls.

At the Brookline High School, whenever a local or national election takes place, the boys and girls hold a corresponding election in a schoolroom, fitted up for the purpose as a polling booth, with proper voting tickets printed by the school. A record is kept of the results by the head master in a special book. This book we examined. It does not appear that any objections are ever made to such methods being used even in the public schools. We were struck by the great skill of the teachers in lessons on civics, in combining enthusiasm and interest for the subjects with absolute impartiality.

Civics at the Pratt Institute High School.—This, a private school in Brooklyn, connected with the great Pratt Institute, has special plans for the teaching of civics. Our attention was first drawn to this by their exhibit in Chicago; we therefore visited the school later, and by the kindness of the head master, were allowed to study the system. The Presidential messages, the Queen's speech, and important Bills of Congress are analysed; the pupils cutting out the text from a newspaper, pasting it on a foolscap sheet, and writing comments and explanations at the side. There is also a special arrangement for interesting the pupils in current events.

We quote from the prospectus :—

" Ten minutes of each day are given to the announcement of the important happenings of the world. A corps of twelve pupil editors, serving a week at a time, take from the morning papers the gist of the news and bulletin it upon blackboards arranged for the purpose in the assembly hall, illustrating when desirable with drawings and maps. These bulletins are read and explained before the whole school, and historical or scientific references are elucidated."

Drawing is used largely for illustration. Rapid blackboard sketching by the pupils of maps, buildings, and the faces of great men is insisted upon. We inspected a large quantity of excellent work of this kind.

The method of recitation from the text-book was, of course, largely used.[1] The lessons thus appeared to be wanting in interest; few, if any, teachers made any attempt to kindle the imagination of the pupils by putting before them an animated sketch of the subject under consideration. It is assumed that the young people can do this for themselves by reading, and that they do not require to be inspired by the teacher's more complete realisation of the past, and by her dramatic power of making it present. We heard very little, too, of any philosophy of history, and consequently the attention of the pupils was not drawn to the ethical lessons

---

[1] See Method, page 77.

which the course of history conveys; but this
omission may have been accidental, occurring only
in the lessons at which the writer was present.

The connection of cause and effect was, however,
clearly brought out by the pupils under that skilful
questioning which is so marked a characteristic
of American teachers. Excellent illustrations from
other periods and countries for comparison and con-
trast were frequently given by pupil or teacher—
generally by the latter. If a debatable point arose,
the argument on both sides was thoroughly well
worked out; in fact, the adjective *legal* might be
applied to the method. The work in every case is
done almost entirely by the pupil, nor was this confined always to the text-books. In the more progressive schools, pupils are regularly set to get up
parts of the subjects from the school library, or even
the public library of the district, as a teacher does
when preparing a lesson. References are given to
them, and they are required to produce the results
of their work, either on paper or orally, by a given
date, for the benefit of the whole class. We heard
and saw some admirable work of this kind. We
recall particularly a lesson in the Coloured High
School in Washington, where part of an essay on
the famous Ordinance of 1787, for the Government
of the North-West Territory, was read by a girl,
who had used the Library of Congress for some of
her material.

This plan is termed the "laboratory method,"
and teachers lay great stress on it; in fact, they
considered their work was not done, unless they had

taught the pupils how to read and how to use a library.

In the High School at Brookline, Mass., some girls were doing original research on the early history of the town. One took the history of the Lyceum (Mechanics' Institute) movement, in 1840; another the question of public conveyances between Brookline and Boston. Another was working up from public documents an essay entitled "Three glimpses of Brookline, 1650, 1700, 1893." By the courtesy of the head master, we were allowed to converse with these girls and to see some of their notes. We understood that they were not preparing for any examination.

In this school we were shown a large portfolio of diagrams, chiefly on squared paper, illustrating taxation and other points of local history, made by the boys and girls.

At Vassar College, the Professor of History,[1] allowed us to see something of her methods of teaching college girls how to do research. Her aim was to train them to perform, one by one, various exercises occurring in the study of history—how to get up a biography, how to argue a disputed point, how to measure historic authorities, etc. For example, the students had been set to find out the causes of the excesses in the French Revolution. They each returned to the Professor a series of cards bearing extracts from different authors, with the reference to the book from which the reference was drawn.

[1] Miss Mary N. Salmon.

In Smith College, Northampton, Mass., we heard a fine lecture on General History delivered by the professor to a large senior class ; but it so closely resembled one given in an English College, or to an advanced class in a High School, as to need no comment.

In the public schools, little illustrative material is provided for lessons in history, though the maps were often good; in some private schools, on the other hand, the material equipment appeared to include nearly all that is yet published for the purpose. At one of these schools where the subjects are all connected together, History is the central subject as dealing with humanity. It determines the geography and literature, and if possible, the science studied. The course at the practising school of the Cook County Normal College, Chicago (Colonel Parker's), is arranged on the same theory of " concentration "—an eight years' course in general history being carefully planned for the children. They study the geography of the continents and the history of Columbus and the Pilgrim Fathers together. They copy examples of historic ornament in their drawing lessons. The Cook County Normal College has an excellent reference library and a large collection of newspaper cuttings, arranged, not in books, but in a patent document file-cabinet.

The study of history in Colleges and Universities in America is far too large a subject to be touched upon here. To a student of history, the methods, appliances, and schemes of work appear extremely attractive ; the great Johns Hopkins Historical

Seminary is particularly impressive. Its motto is, "History is past politics, and politics present history."

In the Massachusetts Institute of Technology, the Professors of History and Economics have elaborated a special method of diagrammatic illustration, which might well be applied to school use. Large sheets of squared paper are used for coloured charts, showing statistical results through a period of years—similar to the barometer and thermometer charts in the daily newspapers, or those used by engineers. Some of the subjects thus treated were:—the prices of United States bonds; English coinage from 1300 to 1600; war expenditure in the United States; pauperism, etc. The Bureau of Education has published a special circular on the Study of History in American Colleges and Universities, by Dr. H. B. Adam, of Johns Hopkins. This gives elaborate accounts of college work with illustrations and tables, and should be read by every one specially interested in the subject.[1] It gives an interesting account of the success of women in the study of history. One of the best known text-books "Studies in General History," is by a woman,—Mary D. Sheldon, a graduate of the University of Michigan.

The Teaching of Science.

American educators universally consider some training in science to be a necessary part of a liberal education; all High School courses include some science work, and many of the best Colleges

---

[1] The Teachers' Guild Library possesses a copy.

and Universities require either chemistry or physics for matriculation; Harvard in particular has fixed a high standard in this respect. One of the most interesting educational movements of the present day in America is the question of science-teaching in the elementary schools. Although this is not strictly within the limits of our subject, we saw and heard so much of it, and American teachers considered it to be of so much importance, that we felt obliged to make a few notes on the matter.

The principle of introducing science into the primary and secondary school course is an essential part of the "new education," to which we referred in the Introduction. One of the best known exponents of it is Colonel Parker, of the Cook County Normal School, Chicago, where the theory of concentration is the foundation of the pedagogic system. "In this theory the subjects of thought and study are the natural sciences, geography, and history; the unity of these subjects is found in the study of life." [1]

Elementary science work in accordance with this principle is the main object of study. The little child is taught to observe natural objects for himself, to express what he learns in speech, modelling, drawing and writing. He then learns to read short sentences about animals, seeds, etc.; thus the work in language, reading and writing is subsidiary to the science work. The interest of the child is aroused, he desires to express himself, and so learns

---

[1] Course of Study of Cook County Normal School.

modes of expression very much more quickly than under the old system ; at the same time he acquires the habits of observing and thinking about the world around him, and receives indirect moral training.

The writer was present at a lesson in reading and writing given to a class of little children at the Cook County Normal School. The work done was wonderful, especially as such good results had been attained in a very short time ; there seemed something magical in the way the children learned to read and write the new words connected with the plants they were studying. There is no distinction at this stage between the different divisions of Natural Science ; the course is arranged according to the seasons. The older children make meteorological and other records of their observations throughout the year.

The head of the Science Department at the Cook County School, Mr. Jackman, has published a book "Nature Study for the Common Schools,"[1] giving a full course of simple science work (September to June),—suited for the common school. In Washington, Dist. of Columbia, and Brookline, Mass., we saw a similar system at work in the elementary schools. At the time of our visit it was spring, and these Washington schoolrooms, with their collections of living buds, sprouting seeds, zoological and mineralogical specimens, collected by the pupils, had a very pleasing effect. The children evidently enjoyed the lessons thoroughly.

---

[1] New York. Holt & Co.

At Brookline, Mass., the teachers come to the High School to receive lessons in science (the subject having only lately been introduced), in method, and in the making of simple apparatus ; this ensures thoroughness, and the plan works extremely well. The power of expression of the children, both in writing and drawing, grows quickly with the stimulus of the science work ; we read some excellent compositions illustrated with diagrams, by pupils of 10 to 13 years of age, which displayed great originality. The delight and joy on the children's faces, during the lessons, cannot easily be forgotten. Temescal, California, sent admirable work of this kind to the Exhibition, showing the combination of science, language study, and drawing.

In Massachusetts generally, elementary lessons in plants, animals, chemistry, physics, physical geography, etc., are given in most of the public schools. Local exhibitions of the pupils' collections, drawings, and compositions are held, and excite warm interest among the parents.

In the High Schools, science is regularly taught, and in all the more progressive cities by the inductive method. Many schools possess admirably fitted laboratories, both for chemistry and physics ; there is a general feeling that physics should be a compulsory subject ; about 200 hours (*i.e.*, 5 hours per week, for the 40 weeks of a school year) being required. We heard several excellent lessons.

At the High School, Ann Arbor, a class of from sixteen to twenty pupils was engaged in measuring the focal length of a lens; they were divided into small groups, each with one piece of apparatus, arranged round an electric lamp burning in the centre of the room. The power for the dynamo was drawn from the wires for the electric street cars outside.

At Brookline we saw the pupils working at the experiment to show nodal lines on vibrating plates in acoustics. The apparatus here was abundant; each student had a pendulum and tuning fork, and we noticed a large number of balances in the chemistry room. At Washington the class had a typewritten syllabus, and made their own note-books of experiments; they were working with resistance coils, and Wheatstone's bridge. Text-books are only used for reference. The High School, Minneapolis, Minn., which we were unfortunately unable to visit, is famous for its physics teaching, which is under the charge of a woman graduate of the great Massachusetts Institute of Technology. The school sent an admirable exhibit to Chicago, which we carefully examined; the drawings were large and good, and the work was evidently all done from experiments by the pupils. The rule was, " in every experiment show materials, facts, operation, conclusion." Other High Schools in Minnesota also sent excellent work.

Chemistry seems to be always studied in the laboratory, the pupils themselves performing the experiments. This, however, is not the case in the Normal Colleges of New York and Philadelphia; these schools possess no laboratories whatever.

The professors give lectures and perform experiments, and the teachers examine the pupils on the subjects by the aid of text-books. The great High School in Brooklyn has as yet no laboratories, but these are to be built.

We do not understand how so much ground is covered in the lessons on chemistry; the syllabuses appear to contain too much to be done thoroughly in the time, especially with experiments.

Botany is studied in some schools, but there is a tendency to take it as part of biology; there is an admirable system of botany-teaching at the Washington High School, in the third year of the science course.[1] The school has a large lecture hall containing cabinets of specimens, a fine series of wall pictures, a room fitted with tables and microscopes, and a propagating room. The class meets four days a week for lectures, and laboratory work; they also visit the Public Botanical Gardens. During the year, each pupil writes 100 description papers, and three observation papers, stating results of original investigation on general subjects.

We heard a lesson to a class of twenty-five girls of 17 to 18 years of age; they were studying the magnolia, and the development of buds. Each girl had on her desk a frame, like a stand for test-tubes, containing little bottles, which held twigs of various trees. in water. These had been there

---

[1] 1st year. Physiology, Physical Geography, Geology
                    (elementary course).
    2nd   „   Physics and Chemistry.
    3rd   „   Botany.

for several days, that the students might personally observe development, etc. ; to judge by their answers they had done this very well. They made rough notes as the lesson proceeded ; their formal note-books, which were written up in pencil at home, contained excellent diagrams and drawings. In order to keep in mind the relation of flowers to thought, an extract from literature regarding plants is daily placed on the blackboard, and copied by the class.

The school programmes seem to us often to in-clude too many sciences. Physiology is compulsory by law in many States ; chemistry, physics, and biology we have mentioned. Some schools teach also zoology, physical geography, geology, and astronomy. The last we consider unsuited for school work at all, as to do it properly demands a fair knowledge of mathematics. At the Normal College, Philadelphia, we heard part of an astronomy lesson which consisted in recitation from a text-book. In the Ann Arbor English course, the student is expected to study five sciences in four years. We cannot but wish, however, that English High Schools had such admirable provision in laboratories and apparatus for the thorough study of science, as there is in American schools.

Some study of science is generally compulsory in those Colleges and Universities in which the choice of subjects is not entirely free. This statement holds for the women's Colleges. Vassar and Smith have a very fine equipment for the study of science ; the Vassar Chemical Laboratory holds 120 students ;

there is a special room for spectrum analysis, a good museum, and a well-fitted biological laboratory ; the biology laboratory at Smith is also well supplied. We did not visit the science building at Bryn Mawr. The observatories at the Colleges are mentioned in Chapter V. We have been informed that some years ago the science teaching in American schools was very poor ; the impulse to improve it came from the Colleges. The science work in a High School is generally under the charge of a College graduate, a specialist. Harvard demands for its matriculation examination, not only practical work from every student, but the presentation of his laboratory note-book, countersigned by the teacher, to show that he has spent a certain time, and gone through a certain series of experiments, in the laboratory. This measure is said to have had great influence in inducing schools to provide laboratories.

CHAPTER V.

UNIVERSITY EDUCATION FOR WOMEN.

IN America as in England, University education for women has been modelled on the system already existing for men. It is therefore necessary before giving an account of Women's Colleges, to say something about the American ideal of University education in general, which differs considerably from that current in England. To do so is however a somewhat presumptuous task; all that is to be said is already in print in Mr. Bryce's great book,[1] in the chapter entitled "The Universities." He there points out that, though there are several hundred bodies entitled by law to give degrees, there are not more than twelve, and perhaps only eight or nine, which are, in the true sense of the term, Universities. There are, however, about thirty or forty smaller foundations which give a good, though limited, college education; below these stand 300 or more which are really schools. We have already classified the Universities in respect to their organization : the intellectual side is now to be discussed.

The English distinction between a College and a University does not obtain in America; there the

---

[1] See chap. ci.

words are used indiscriminately for degree-giving bodies. The more precise writers, however, are endeavouring to introduce a more accurate terminology, using the word College of an institution giving a general preparatory education in the liberal arts, and the word University, in its true sense, of a great corporation devoted to the advancement of knowledge, whose students have already attained intellectual manhood. We shall not attempt to observe this distinction in the following pages ; we shall rather use the words college education and university education as synonymous. In America, however, the question of this differentiation in higher education is one of extreme importance : on it depends the whole future of the smaller Colleges. They must either sink into being secondary schools, or, remaining as Colleges, act as stepping stones to the Universities proper for those students who will become scholars indeed. This question does not however concern women's Colleges so particularly that we need enter into detail respecting it. The course of study which we shall now consider is a more vital matter.

The American ideal is to give the undergraduate some general culture, to introduce him to all the chief departments of study, to teach him something of each ; in order, first, that he may receive the training which each gives (it being assumed that each subject trains a particular part of the mind); and, second, that he may be able to specialize later, when he has found out his own particular aptitude. Another reason was also given to the writer by an

American educator ; namely, that in a new country where men change their occupations easily, where new problems constantly press on them, and where, as in frontier life, division of labour is not thoroughly organized, versatility and a general knowledge are more important than scholarship and a thorough acquaintance with one subject. Be that as it may, the fact remains that specialization is not regarded with favour in America, except among a few. Originally classics, mathematics, and philosophy were the staple of a college course ; but when science, modern languages, economics, etc., claimed a place in the curriculum, it became clear that some choice must be allowed. No human being could learn all these subjects in the four years of a college course. So began the system of electives—that is, students were allowed to choose some subjects, greater liberty being given in the later years of the course, and a certain amount of classics, mathematics, science, and English being generally required. This system of certain pre-scribed and certain elective subjects still widely prevails, the women's Colleges following it to a greater or less extent.

A student of one of the English Universities is not likely to be favourably impressed by this sys-tem ; it appears to encourage superficiality, and to fritter away time, while the student can never acquire that sense of the vastness of knowledge and the arduousness of really good work, which is one of the greatest advantages of a university education. There is, however, an admirable custom

of " post-graduate work " in all the best Colleges in
America which provides for the scholar, as the
ordinary system provides for the average person.
Mature students who have taken a degree (often in
another and, it may be, an inferior institution) come
to the greater seats of learning to study one subject,
and to learn how to pursue original investigation.
Such work may be compared in standard with what
is done for the triposes at the University of Cambridge ; but, as it is not limited by any examination, it is free, and partakes more largely of the
character of research. For the sake of post-graduate
study, and for other reasons, students often work at
two or even more Universities, as in Germany. In
some places the work done in one institution will
count towards a degree in another. The poorer
Colleges thus have an important work in reaching
persons who, but for their influence, might never
obtain any higher education at all, and who may be
stimulated to go on to a real University, when once
they have tasted the sweets of learning.

The objections to the system of so much prescribed and so much elective work are so strongly
felt in some quarters that two other systems have
been elaborated. One is the " group " system, first
worked out at Johns Hopkins, and adopted for
women at Bryn Mawr. It allows some specialization,
combining subjects in groups of two : we give a
fuller account of it in describing Bryn Mawr. The
other is the pure elective system of Harvard, which
permits of absolute freedom of choice, demanding
for the B.A. degree a certain quantity of work

(twelve courses in four years, each course meaning three lectures a week for a year) and a fixed standard of attainment; but allowing the student to select what subjects he may prefer. Thus he may specialize entirely, as at Cambridge, England, or he may specialize in two subjects, as at Johns Hopkins (with the advantage that he can arrange his groups for himself), or he may follow a course of general culture.

The development of the elective system at Harvard has provoked much comment in America. Some educators dread the danger of choice for young people, and many institutions would find their resources strained if they were not able to insist on many students taking a particular subject, and were not thus able to teach more economically. The matter is discussed at length in a series of articles in the *Andover Review*,[1] by Professor Palmer, of Harvard, head of the department of philosophy. It is perhaps presumptuous in a stranger to give an opinion ; but the principles of University education must be very much the same in one country as in another. We therefore venture to say that the women's Colleges might do well to follow the lead of the oldest College in the New World, that daughter of the Cambridge beyond seas, " singularly beautiful, reverend in its age, magnificent in its endowments, equable in its working," which stands in the van of education and progress in America, and which an Englishman can hardly contemplate without a thrill of admiration, it may be even of love.

---

[1] *Andover Review*, 1886.

Another marked difference between the American and the English University systems is found in the conditions for a degree. The stress here is on residence and examinations at the older Universities, and on examinations at the newer. There the stress is on attendance at a certain number of lectures, given by professors or other members of the faculty of the College or University. The teachers may, and we believe generally do, examine their own students, and they, of course, exact a certain quantity of work from them while attending lectures, either in the form of paper work or of oral recitations. The professor reports a man as having gone through a certain course, and so many courses of a certain kind are required for a degree. Thus in all schemes of work the number of hours of lecture per week appear in a prominent position. All students are however examined on entrance, unless they bring certificates which excuse the examination. There is little if any difference between honour and pass men, and, as Mr. Bryce says, "At no point in his (the student's) career is he expected to submit to any examination comparable, for the combined number and difficulty of the subjects in which he is questioned, to the final honour examinations at Oxford and Cambridge." [1]

The most important institutions giving a College education to women are the separate women's Colleges, founded by private munificence, having their own charters to give degrees, and their own

---

[1] Vol. ii. p. 555.

independent staff of teachers, the head being in almost every case a man. The four largest and most esteemed of these are Vassar, Wellesley, Smith, and Bryn Mawr ; of these we give separate accounts below. The great Universities and Colleges for men have not been as a rule open to women, though at the present time signs of a change are clearly visible. Thus "annexes" have grown up at Harvard, Cambridge, and Columbia, New York.[1] These are organizations for giving women the College education men have at these seats of learning. Some of the privately endowed Universities recently founded are, however, open to women on exactly the same conditions as to men ; the chief of these is Cornell, Ithaca, New York. We much regret that time did not allow of our visiting this institution, one of the most important in connection with the question of co-education. The new University of Chicago has followed the example of Cornell. The Western State Universities are also open to women ; chief among these is the University of Michigan, described in the next chapter, which has influenced the University education of women in America more than any other institution.

There is much discussion among American educators as to whether it is better to send a girl to a separate women's College, or to a co-education University, and public opinion is very strong on both sides ; the matter does not turn on the question of securing the highest and most advanced teaching, though that is considered, but rather on social

---

[1] The Annex here is termed Barnard College.

conditions.   Some persons object to the conventual
character of the women's Colleges, isolated as they
are from the outside world ; others think the calm and
freedom from the distractions of social life a positive
advantage.   We shall, however, discuss this more
fully in the chapter on Co-education.

There is at least one other great institution
admitting women which, though not strictly a
University, for it gives no instruction in ancient
languages, is yet of very high rank and of great
importance—we mean the Massachusetts Institute of
Technology.   It grants the B.Sc. degree, and women
have studied there for some years, principally natural
science and economics; some have studied architecture.

All the chief women's Colleges require an entrance
examination somewhat similar to the Matriculation
Examination of the University of London, but not
so difficult.   Vassar, Wellesley, and Smith accept
the certificates of certain schools as substitutes for
the examination ; Bryn Mawr recognizes no school
certificate, only that of the Harvard examinations for
women being taken.   Girls seem to enter at about
the same age as in England, possibly on the whole
when somewhat younger; 16 is the limit fixed
by the college authorities.   The students seem as
mature in appearance and demeanour as our English
college women, but the American Colleges themselves seem rather to resemble boarding schools.
The whole morning is taken up with recitations, as
in school; the girls have little free time, the rules
prescribe retiring to rest at a fixed hour, etc.; there

is a weekly holiday, Saturday or Monday, and exeats for the week end are easily and frequently obtained. Some Colleges adopt the cottage system, wholly or in part ; the students live in small groups, each under the charge of one lady, who is in the position of a mother. There is something very sweet and beautiful in these little homes ; they are doubtless of the greatest value in making College life possible for a certain type of girl.

We heard much from some American educators of the exciting, and in some cases injurious, effect of a large number of girls living together in one building. This was said to generate an atmosphere of nervous excitement, the noise of the crowded dining hall at meals being particularly bad. The influence of the mass of so many young women on one another was also considered by some to be hurtful, the conditions being so different from home life. We were not able to understand this objection, but there must be some weight in it, for persons of experience and standing urge it strongly ; the point seems to be that such a system is unnatural, and therefore necessarily bad.

The material equipment is much the same in all the principal institutions ; it is on the whole very much finer than anything in England, though none of the buildings for women are as splendid as those of Holloway College. The quadrangle plan is rarely used in America, detached buildings being better suited to the cold and snows of their winter.[1] A more particular description is given under the separate headings ; all have good libraries, which are

---

[1] Bryce, vol. ii. p. 551.   I

extensively used. Smith relies also on the public library of Northampton, which is peculiarly good. All have observatories, well fitted with instruments, on which no expense has been spared; here some of the students work regularly. The opportunities for physical training are described in Chapter VII. Everything possible in reason seems to be done for the comfort of students; we were struck with the uniform excellence of the food served at meals.

The relations of the students with the authorities are marked by great friendliness, and by the absence of any stiffness or formality. This we noticed again and again, while going over the buildings with members of the faculty, waiting in offices during the transaction of business, at table, and elsewhere. The life of the Colleges left on the writer's mind a peculiar impression of restful pleasantness, something of the feeling of a home. *Wellesley*, with its beautiful grounds, its seclusion, its art treasures, its traditions, has a spirit of its own, difficult to express in words, but felt by one who visits it. *Bryn Mawr* recalls Girton, though it is in many respects different. *Vassar* is majestic; its grounds have the dignity of fine trees and wide lawns; its wealth harmonizes with that of the Empire State (New York) in which it is situated. *Smith* seemed to the writer to have the characteristics attributed in literature to New England. The morning service in its spacious but simple chapel, where 700 students meet, is singularly impressive.

We feel, however, very strongly on one point, and after discussing the matter with some American authorities, we venture to make an adverse criticism : the required attendance on lectures is far too large in number of hours. In most Colleges *fifteen* hours a week is the rule ; some allow more, even twenty hours per week being taken. To an English student it appears necessary to devote at least six hours preparation, and often more, to every hour of lecture. This would mean ninety hours private work, which, with the lectures, would make 105 hours per week, *i.e.,* seventeen and a half hours per day. This is of course absurd ; we therefore conclude that the standard of preparation is not so high as in England. The authorities themselves state that about *two* hours per lecture is expected ; this would give an eight hours day. But a College lecture which only requires two hours preparation can hardly be considered to reach the standard of University work at all. We must accept, therefore, one of two alternatives : the students are overworked, or the work done is not of a very advanced character. When we remember that students are often admitted at 16 years of age, we can take the latter explanation. But it would be in the highest degree unjust to suppose that in the best Colleges the standard is, as a rule, low.

The writer would suggest that, in the women's Colleges at all events, the students must, to do justice to their instruction, work long hours, though some of the work is not of a very intense kind. This *à priori* conclusion was borne out by some of the phenomena we observed on visiting the women's Colleges. In one we were informed that it was very difficult to get the students to avail themselves of the opportunities for physical exercise, they never seemed to have any time. As lectures were given both morning and afternoon, and as the time between had to be filled with reading, laboratory work, etc., we could understand that the custom of devoting the early afternoon to physical exercise, as at Cambridge, could not well be followed. In two other Colleges we were told that great stress was laid on the observance of the rule of retiring to rest at 10 p.m. This would be unnecessary if the students had more free time, as they would probably then find out for themselves how to fit in their work without sitting up late. We were struck by the absence of all allusion to that social life among the students in their own rooms, which forms so important a part of English College life among women, does so much to develop self-reliance and thought on subjects apart from study, and indeed helps so materially towards that maturing of character which is the most important result of the years spent at College.

Such social life may exist in American Colleges ; our stay was too short to enable us to be positive on the subject, but we heard nothing of it, and we could not see where the time for it was to be found. The arrangement of rooms, too, in some buildings, would hinder the rise of such a system. The English ideal, that each student should have her own domain, one room or two, does not generally prevail. A common rule is to have rooms in suites, two bedrooms and one sitting-room ; in the main building at Vassar, three bedrooms go to each sitting-room. In some Colleges two students share a bedroom and a sitting-room. Such arrangements lend themselves to the formation of College friendships, also an important part of College life, but we cannot but feel that to put each student by herself, to let her live alone and work alone for some portion of the day, and to give her opportunities of receiving her friends in her own rooms, much as ladies do in their houses, tends to develop the individual character, and to change the school-girl into a woman.

When we consider how much freer the discipline of American schools is than that customary in England, it seems strange that College life there should offer so narrow a field for the self-direction of the individual. We feel as certain as a stranger can venture to be that the cause of this is the exaction of fifteen hours per week attendance on lectures. Any experienced teacher can understand that quite as much advanced work might be done in fewer hours. Indeed, the students would then do more, as they would have more time for study. They would also enjoy what is, in the writer's opinion, one of the greatest privileges of English College life among women—time to think. In the family the girl has home duties; her school days are filled with varying occupations; on leaving College she will have to satisfy the claims of practical and professional life, or of society. The period between school and adult life, spent as it is apart from the family, in comparative solitude and independence, is the time for the growth and maturity of the inner nature.

" Es bildet ein Talent sich in der Stille." [1]

---

[1] Goethe.

Such a privilege, it seems to us, few American College girls can ever enjoy.

THE HARVARD ANNEX.
(The Society for the Collegiate Instruction of Women.)

As has before been stated, this institution is not a College for women; it is rather an organization for giving to women the same collegiate instruction as that which men receive at Harvard. Both from its unique character, and from the fact that it has been called the American Girton, it has seemed to us to demand a somewhat detailed report.

About the year 1876, the thought came to the originators of the plan that a systematic arrangement might be made by which women could receive instruction from the Professors of Harvard College. There were two objections to admitting women to the men's classes, even had Harvard been ready to admit them ; one was the feeling against " the mingling of the sexes in the college rooms," the other is characteristic of that conservative respect for the ancient forms of law in America, which Mr. Bryce remarks upon.[1] It is the doubt " as to the legal propriety of admitting women to privileges which had been endowed for men, and had been for more than two centuries administered solely for them." After much deliberation and consultation with some of the Harvard professors, a plan was formed, chiefly through the efforts of Mr. and Mrs. Gilman, and a directing body (now termed, The Society for the Collegiate Instruction of Women) was formed, con-

---

[1] Vol. ii., p. 504.

sisting of seven ladies and the secretary. By February, 1879, a circular was issued, and applications for admission were soon received. In September entrance examinations were held, coinciding exactly with those for young men, and the first year began with twenty-five students, who formed twenty-nine classes and brought into service twenty-three of the Harvard teachers. Lecture rooms were provided in a private house; the Annex has never established a dormitory (what would be called in England a hall of residence) for its students. The managers have preferred arrangements for lodging in private families offered for the purpose.

The number of pupils soon increased so considerably, that it became necessary to fit up a complete building for lectures, and Fay House, a place with historic memories, standing almost beneath the shadow of the venerable Washington elm, was offered to the society, and opened about 1886. It has since been enlarged, and now forms a centre for social life among the students, as well as a shelter for the actual teaching. The society has become a regular corporation, with nineteen members, eight women—including Mrs. Agassiz, widow of the great Agassiz, and Miss Alice Longfellow,—and eleven men, several of whom are eminent Harvard professors. Mr. Gilman is still the secretary as at the beginning. There are now 241 students, 22 being graduates of other colleges, taught by 74 of the instructors of Harvard College ; these instructors repeat to the women students the identical lectures which they give to the men.

As stated above, the test of a University course in America is not an examination, but attendance on lectures: the Annex is therefore obliged to have Harvard professors only. It cannot employ a woman, however distinguished, unless she is on the Harvard staff.[1] In this respect Girton and Newnham, and the Oxford Colleges for women, are free to employ any instructor without lowering their standard; the University examination is the test, not the attendance at the lectures of any particular teacher. There is some misapprehension on this point in America, some persons thinking that the Harvard Annex complies more completely with the Harvard regulations for men than Girton or Newnham do with the requirements of the University of Cambridge. At Girton the requirements are, and always have been, identically the same as the University requirements for men.

The current Calendar of the Annex offers courses in all the more important subjects of university education; 302 students study English, which is required by Harvard College in the Freshman year —this accounts partly for its predominance. Classics stands next, then history; the unpopularity of mathematics is striking, only twenty-four students taking it. The collections of the Agassiz and other museums of Harvard are open to the students, and by the vote of the President and Fellows they have free use of the great library, which contains 360,000 volumes. Opportunities for study in the

---

[1] There are, of course, no such women.

Astronomical Observatory and the Botanic Garden are also offered.

The requirements for admission are those of the Harvard examinations for women; special students who desire to take certain courses, and students of mature age who wish to pursue higher courses of study, are admitted at the discretion of the authorities.

Massachusetts furnishes by far the largest percentage of students (73·8%), after it comes New York (6·2%). Private schools prepare the majority (42·4%) ; but the High Schools of New England absorb a large number (37·6%), the Cambridge High and Latin Schools sending more than any other institution—29 out of 241. The total percentage for High Schools all over the States is 40·1.

The regulations declare that " Any student who, having passed the regular examination for admission, has pursued with success a four years' course of study such as would be accepted for the degree of Bachelor of Arts in Harvard College, will be entitled to a certificate to that effect." It appears, however, that few comply with these conditions, only 10 out of 241 receiving the B.A. certificate in 1892. This is one striking difference between the Annex and Girton College; at the latter institution nearly all the students fulfil the University requirements for the B.A. degree in Honours. Another difference is the absence of college life.

Fay House, with its fine reception rooms and beautiful library, affords occasions for corporate life to students ; they have several clubs for social enjoy-

ment and discussion.   The writer attended an afternoon reception given by the Idler Club, which was
characterized by all that charm and grace which
have made the social gifts of American women
famous everywhere.   The afternoon teas held by
Mrs. Agassiz weekly in Fay House during the
season afford an agreeable means of bringing together the students and their friends, and of making
them acquainted with the professors, the ladies of
the Corporation, and others.

The fees are £15 a year for one course, and £40
for three courses or more.   The endowment is comparatively small; it is clear therefore that such
advanced instruction could not be secured except by
the most watchful care and devotion on the part of
the officers of the society, and by the practical
sympathy and kindness of the Harvard professors
and instructors.

One or two scholarships are given, and several
prizes.   There is a fund for printing monographs
written by the students, chiefly on historical and
biographical subjects.

The average entrance of Freshmen is 17·3 years
of age; the graduate students average 28·5.   Many
of the alumnæ are engaged in teaching, the Annex
holding, of course, a very high place in popular
esteem.   It seems to fill a special function in giving
advanced students special instruction in some one
branch for a year or more, thus qualifying them for
posts in observatories and other departments of work
in women's Colleges.[1]

---

[1] See " The Harvard Annex, the Story of its Beginning
and Growth."   Cambridge, 1891.

The future of the Annex is full of interest; its relation to Harvard cannot long continue on the present indefinite footing. What may happen is, of course, uncertain; but for English people there is probably no place of collegiate instruction for women in America so attractive. The movement for the University education of women in England has been so completely identified with the older institutions for men, that their interest naturally attaches itself to the effort to extend to women the privileges of the most venerable and magnificent of American seats of learning.

Vassar, Poughkeepsie, New York.

Vassar is, in the strict sense of the term, the oldest women's College in the United States. It was founded by Matthew Vassar in 1861, and opened in 1866.

The College had to face a good deal of ridicule and opposition at first, but now holds a recognized place. Other benefactors have added to the endowment provided for it by the founder; a new model building for the residence of students, well designed and beautifully decorated, was just being finished at the time of our visit. There are 430 students with a faculty of 41—twelve being men. Students are admitted after passing the usual entrance examination, or on producing certificates from schools approved by a committee of the faculty, the certificates of the Regents of the University of the State of New York, or the certificate of the Harvard examination for women. The chief feature of the regular course is the insistence on two languages (one of which must be Latin) being studied for two years. Music and art may be studied as well as academic subjects. The fee for tuition, board, lodging, and washing is £80—music and art being extra. Large sums are devoted to scholarships for students who need aid.

Vassar has one main building, lofty and long (500 feet), with the new hall of residence near. It has also a well fitted science building, the gift of Vassar Brothers ; a fund provides apparatus, so that its facilities for science are great. Like the other colleges, it has its own observatory, with high-class instruments which are regularly used by the students. The collections in its museums are exceptionally fine; many a large city might be proud to have its art gallery and its hall of casts. The latter contains specimens of all the great periods of sculpture—the Venus of Milo, the Ghiberti Gates, etc., the same size as the originals, as well as forty-two Tanagra figures.

The library contains 19,000 volumes; the reading-room receives the chief newspapers and periodicals, scientific, philological, and literary, in English, French, and German. The museum has 10,000 mineralogical specimens,—5,000 fossils, including some vertebrates of the Tertiary Period from the Bad Lands of Nebraska, collected by an expert employed for two years by the College—and a magnificent series of zoological specimens, including the famous Giraud collection of North American birds. Best of all, however, are the grounds, park-like and extensive, and carefully laid out. We were, unfortunately, unable to hear any lectures, as the college was *en fête*, celebrating Founder's Day, when we visited it ; but this circumstance only strengthened the impression of stateliness and beauty which the College conveys.

Smith College, Northampton, Mass.

Smith College was founded in 1875 by Miss Sophia Smith, with the object of establishing an institution for the higher education of young women, which should give them means and facilities for education equal to those in Colleges for young men. It has three courses of study : the classical, leading to the degree of B.A. ; the scientific, to that of B.Sc. (Bachelor of Science); and the literary, to that of B.L. (Bachelor of Literature). Art and music are also studied. It is difficult to describe these courses without giving elaborate details, as so many subjects are required. Electives are allowed, especially in the later years, to be selected from a very complete list, which contains the usual academic subjects, art, and music.

The number of students is 696, ten being graduates. The faculty numbers thirty-four, with nine non-resident lecturers. The tuition fee is $100 (£20), and that for board and residence $250 (£50). The students have no domestic work except " the care of their own rooms." There is a fair provision for scholarships, loans, etc., for meritorious students.

Northampton is a large village among the hills of the Connecticut Valley, beautifully situated and picturesquely built, its streets shaded with large trees. The college buildings stand in the centre of the village, scattered about over a small park. There is one very large building, containing the chapel, recitation rooms, etc., and a special science building, very well equipped, with good chemical and biological laboratories.

Many of the college students engage in teaching after their college course is over; the phrase, "a graduate of Smith," is quoted in speaking of a woman on the staff of a High School, as if it conveyed a special qualification. From this and other indications we infer that the College takes a high place in public estimation.

Wellesley College.

Wellesley College was established in 1875 by Henry Durant, at Wellesley, fifteen miles west of Boston, on a fine estate of 300 acres, including a large lake, Lake Waban. The College has always been intended not simply to give a liberal education, but to aid in the formation of character. The influences of the natural beauty of the surroundings, and of the art treasures, accumulated in great part by the founder himself, are looked upon as the means to this end. So also is the general spirit of the college life. As the Calendar states: "The College is undenominational, but distinctly and positively Christian in its influence, discipline, and instruction. The systematic study of the Bible is required. Daily services are held in the chapel. The Sunday services are conducted by ministers of different denominations." The students show great interest in philanthropic and missionary work, supporting two special missionaries. The students' Christian Association numbers 460. Distinguished persons visiting the College give lectures from time to time on subjects of general interest, more particularly theology and social reform.

The main building (475 ft. by 510 ft., and five storeys high), which accommodates more than 300 students, and contains a large chapel, library, dining hall, laboratories, lecture rooms, etc., stands on a hill by the side of Lake Waban. In the grounds is another hall, accommodating more than 100 students, and six cottages, holding from fifty to ten students, so that those for whom life among a large number is unsuitable, can live in comparative retirement. There is also a fine School of Art (a special gift), with studios, and the nucleus of an art collection. The music building is near, with its thirty-eight music rooms, and a hall for concerts. The site of the College is ideal; the various buildings, grouped among lawns and fragments of the original forest, and crowning the natural elevations of the ground, form a beautiful whole, different from anything we associate with Colleges in England, but with a charm and grace peculiarly its own.

The President's Report gives an interesting account of the work of the alumnæ (old students) during the thirteen years which have passed since the first class graduated from the College. "Of these 734 graduates, 540 have engaged in educational work, 134 have married, 23 have died, 12 hold the medical degree and are practising physicians, 15 are trained librarians, 9 have engaged in foreign, and 11 in home missionary work. Many of the whole number are in conspicuous positions of responsibility."

The whole number of students at the date of the last report (1892) is 700; a large number who applied for admission were debarred for want of room. The officers of the College number 92, 77 being engaged in teaching.   Wellesley is remarkable for having had from the beginning a woman for its President, and its staff is composed almost entirely of women. By the munificence of a special benefactor, the teachers enjoy what is termed a "Sabbatical Year"; that is, they can spend each seventh year in study or rest. Most come to England for this purpose. Students are admitted on examination, or "on certificate."   The college courses are two: Classical and Scientific, leading respectively to the degrees of B.A. and B.Sc. So much required work and so much elective, amounting to fourteen to sixteen hours a week, is the rule. The proportion of students obtaining a degree is unusually high. In 1891 there were 123 graduates.   Very few students do post-graduate work at Wellesley, only ten appearing, out of 700, in the last list.

Although the College has no large endowment, the fees are low, tuition being $150 (£30), and board and residence amounting to $200 (£40); music and art are extras. There is considerable provision for scholarships and loans for girls who would otherwise be unable to obtain an education.

The writer spent a day and a night at Wellesley College, and had some opportunity of seeing the life of the place, and formed a very favourable impression of it. The relations between the authorities and the students seemed particularly cordial and friendly; the girls, in spite of the somewhat long hours of work, were bright and happy-looking, and the atmosphere of refinement and kindliness was peculiarly delightful.

The College has had from the beginning a fine library, which now contains between 40,000 and 50,000 volumes, and it has an endowment which provides for its increase. The room itself resembles the library of one of our old English Colleges, and contains an interesting series of portraits and autographs of distinguished men, Americans and English. The College also possesses a valuable and unique collection of books and MSS. in the North American Indian languages (the Powell Library). The laboratories are inadequate to their purpose, but the rapid growth of the College has somewhat strained its resources. It needs a science building where the laboratory work could be carried on more thoroughly, and which could be isolated from the dwellings. Doubtless before long public munificence will provide for this and other pressing requirements of an institution which is doing such admirable work for so large a number of young women.

Bryn Mawr, near Philadelphia.

This College, although it is only eight years old, having been opened in the autumn of 1885, has

K

already taken a very high place among the women's Colleges. It has laid itself out to give advanced instruction, and has thus a large number of graduate students, three of them being certificated students of Girton College, two wranglers, and one who took a first class in the classical tripos. This fact gives English people a convenient standard from which to estimate the character of the instruction given at Bryn Mawr. The faculty consists of men and women of very high standing, including graduates of the great German Universities, Zurich, Johns Hopkins, Harvard, Cambridge (England), a distinguished Newnham student, and the only woman who has taken the D.Sc. in mathematics at the University of London. There are 38 instructors, and 194 students, 32 being graduates, doing postgraduate work. Several of these are Fellows of the College; their position is of special interest (there not being anything to exactly correspond to it in our English Colleges). One of the fellowships—that in Greek—is held by the Girton student of classics mentioned above.[1]   The regulations state :—

"The most distinguished place among graduate students will be held by the Fellows, who must reside in the College during the academic year. Nine fellowships, of the value of five hundred and twenty-five dollars each, are awarded annually. They are open to graduates of Bryn Mawr College, or of any other College of good standing."

Undergraduates are required to pass the Bryn Mawr entrance examination, which appears to be nearly equivalent to the Matriculation Examination

---

[1] Another is held in mathematics by a Girton student (1894).

of the University of London. The only exemption allowed is the Harvard certificate in equivalent, or a certificate from a College or University of acknowledged standing. Private schools prepare the majority of students. In the current calendar the proportion from private schools is 79·8 per cent.; other Colleges and Universities send 9·8 per cent., and High Schools only 8 per cent.; the rest (2·4 per cent.) were prepared by private study.

The course for the B.A. degree requires some English, science—or science and history—and philosophy. This only occupies part of the time; the rest must be given to the "Group" selected by the student. The group system is borrowed from the course at the Johns Hopkins University, Baltimore. It is intended to allow some degree of specialization, with provision for width of view by combining subjects. Five groups are arranged as follows: 1. Any language with any language. 2. Any science with any science. 3. Mathematics with Greek and Latin. 4. Mathematics with Physics. 5. History, with Political Science.

The College is situated near Philadelphia (10 miles distant), in grounds of forty acres. There is a main building devoted to lecture rooms, etc., and a separate science hall and gymnasium. The students reside in three separate halls, each with its own kitchens, dining-room, etc., and each under the charge of a mistress. The President of the College is a man, but the Dean of the Faculty—a woman—has, of course, a very large share in the management of the College. The fee for tuition is $100

(£20), for board $150 (£30); room rent varies, according to the room or rooms taken—from $125 (£25) to $250 (£50). Thus the total charge is from £75 to £100. There is a fine library, on which £600 is spent annually for books. 172 periodicals are taken. It includes the library of M. Arniaud, of Paris, the eminent Assyriologist.

Massachusetts Institute of Technology.

This magnificent institution, perhaps the most remarkable in Boston, was founded in 1861 and opened in 1865. It is a University of Industrial Science. The greater part of its work is outside the scope of the present inquiry, the great majority of its graduates being men preparing for the various engineering professions. It is, however, open to women, who there study architecture, history, and economics, and above all science. The designer of the Woman's Building at the Chicago Exhibition received her training here. The Institute occupies a large number of buildings, the two most important being the "Rogers" and the "Walker" buildings, — prominent architectural features of the best quarter of Boston. In them are the large laboratories, fitted in the most complete manner; 625 students can be accommodated at once in the chemical section.

Central and fundamental in its curriculum are thorough introductory courses in Mathematics, Chemistry, and Physics. There are twelve complete courses, each of four years' duration, by which the degree of B.Sc. is given; many women have prepared themselves to be teachers of science, the degree having a very high value. A rigid matriculation examination is required. The work in sanitary science, which is in great part under the direction of a lady, Mrs. Ellen H. Richards, is followed by women who intend to teach domestic science in schools. The equipment for the study of history and economics is very elaborate; what are termed "laboratory methods" are largely used, *i.e.*, the students do original work for themselves in the library; there are two courses in statistics. The President of the institution, we may remark, is General Francis A. Walker, the economist.

University of Chicago.

This University is a striking example both of the American enthusiasm for education and of the munificence of their wealthy men towards it. As Chicago hopes (it is said) to be one day the greatest commercial centre of the United States, perhaps of the world, she must needs have a great University to maintain intellectual and spiritual ideals against the influence of materialism. Such an institution is now being actually established by the continued force of a group of wealthy and eminent citizens and of the body of deans and professors, who have been brought together from all the great Universities of the world. Its history deserves a note, as illustrating the power of voluntary and private effort in education. In 1889 the American Baptist Education Society decided to establish a well equipped College in Chicago; subscriptions poured in, the work developed, and in 1890 a charter was obtained for a University. John D. Rockefeller took so prominent a part in the movement, giving a very large proportion of the endowment (now more than £1,000,000 sterling), that his name now stands as that of the founder. Two-thirds of the trustees and the president must be Baptists, but there is no other religious test or limitation; four blocks on one of the parks on the south side were obtained, occupying about twenty-four acres, and buildings of grey stone in the English University style, somewhat resembling the new part of Caius College, Cambridge, have been erected. When complete the University will be as beautiful (and more enduring) than the White City of the World's Fair. The president is William R. Harper, Ph.D., late Professor of Semitic languages at Yale; the staff numbers 189 already. No instructor is required to lecture more than thirty-six weeks per year (ten to twelve hours a week). There are now [1] about 700 students, but as the buildings are finished more will come; women are admitted on equal terms, there is a special hall of residence for them, and a woman as dean; 23% of the students are women. Fellowships are given liberally. The session has four quarters, each of three months, and a student is usually only allowed to take three quarters in the year; the courses are complete in themselves, and thus a student can earn his or her living during part of the year, and in time complete the whole work for a degree.

The University extension work is of great interest;

[1] June, 1893.

the faculty numbers fifty, who lecture in Illinois and the neighbouring States; sociological work and University settlements are also to be founded.

The eminence of the names on the list of professors shows clearly that the University of Chicago is intended to be one of the great educational institutions of the United States;—to see this University in the making, not by fiat of the State, but by individual effort, not across the mists of tradition and antiquity, but in the clear daylight of the modern world, was as remarkable an experience as could well fall to the lot of an inquirer.

CHAPTER VI

THIS University may be taken as a type of the State Universities, which are the only institutions of higher education in America, that form part of the State system. It is by far the largest and most important of all these; indeed the statistics for it and for the University of Minnesota, in the Bureau of Education Report, stand out conspicuously in respect to the number of students, wealth, and equipment. The State Universities which have been established in all the Western, and some of the South Western States, are modelled to a considerable degree on this University. It is also noteworthy as one of the first great institutions to open its doors to women, and it has thus had an important influence on the whole question of women's education. The system of admitting "on certificate" from High Schools to the Universities also originated here; on these grounds the writer has deemed it advisable to devote a chapter to this institution, which touches at several points the subject of the present inquiry.

When the Congress of the United States, after the conclusion of the War of Independence, laid down an Ordinance for the Government of the

North-West Territory, it declared : — " Religion, morality, and knowledge being necessary to good government and the happiness of mankind, schools and the means of education shall for ever 'be encouraged." Michigan was one of the districts formed from this territory; in accordance with the Ordinance, a certain amount of land was reserved for the purpose of maintaining a University. This is the origin of the University of Michigan, and the sentence quoted above is placed upon the walls of its chief building.

The original plan as drawn in 1817 was remarkably broad, though its language was pedantic. In what was termed the "Catholepistemiad," or University of Michigania, the President and Professors of the University were to have the entire direction of collegiate, secondary, and lower education. This plan was however not carried out, but the educational system of Michigan has always been characterized by a remarkable degree of unity. In 1837 the newly settled district had grown populous enough to be admitted as one of the States of the Union ; and the University proper was founded in the same year. Many of the men who framed its first constitution were from New England, themselves College graduates, and were zealous for higher education. One of them, Isaac E. Crary, had made a study of Cousin's famous Report on the Prussian System of Education, and the University of Michigan was from the first modelled on the German system. Its government is by a Board of Regents ; there are now eight of these elected by popular vote for terms of eight years, as provided in the Constitution of the State. For many years the only resources of the University were the public lands already referred to ; these had been mismanaged, and the work of the University was thereby limited. In 1867 the State Legislature voted money from the public treasury ; in March, 1893, the Legislature increased this grant to one-sixth of a mil on each dollar of taxable property, which gives an income of £40,000, on the present valuation. This shows clearly the close bond between the State and the University.

The number of students in all departments is 2,778 (in 1893). No charge is made for tuition, the only fees being the matriculation and incidental expenses (library, etc.) ; persons who do not reside in the State are required to pay rather more than Michigan students. There are no dormitories; the students live where and how they please. The reasons given for this are, first, that the University has not then to deal with questions of internal discipline, and second, that the aggregation of young people in large numbers under one roof is an artificial condition and has injurious influences. The University of Michigan in this resembles those of Germany or Scotland. It has six departments, to all of which women are admitted on equal terms. They are :—1. General Department, *i.e.*, Literature, Science, and the Arts. 2. Medicine and Surgery. 3. Law. 4. Pharmacy. 5. Homeopathic Medical College. 6. Dental Surgery. It is unnecessary to enter into details as to the courses of study ; 1,491 students are entered for the General Department, some of these studying for special subjects and others working for a degree. About one-half of the degree course consists of required subjects, and the rest of optional.

The system of admission " on certificate " from the High Schools, as the German Universities receive students from the Gymnasia, originated in Michigan, and is often termed " the Michigan Method." It was begun in 1870, and is considered to have been very successful. The schools which appeal for this privilege must fulfil three conditions ; their courses of study must be those prescribed by the University, they are periodically inspected by some member of that University, and they receive the privilege of sending up pupils " on certificate," only for a specified time (three years). If their pupils are found to have been insufficiently prepared, the privilege is withdrawn. The faculty have approved of 110 schools, nearly all public High Schools in the State of Michigan : the result of this diploma system are stated to have been as follows :—

1. The bond between University and High School has been strengthened ; graduates of the University have taught in greater numbers in the schools, and the principals of these latter have been consulted by the University about changes of programme.

2. Local interest in secondary education has been stimulated, and the schools have been better equipped ; incompetent teachers have been dismissed, etc.

3. The grade of instruction in the secondary

schools has been raised a whole year during the
twenty years that this system has prevailed.   In
other words, students now entering have had from
the schools what is equivalent to an extra year of
training, though their age is not altered.

As is stated above, this system prevails generally
in the West.   Some Eastern authorities strongly object to it, but the Michigan professors consider it far
better than any other plan.   The *University Record*,
an official publication, states,—"So far as theory is
concerned, it is the simple truth that the creditable
completion of a prescribed course of study in a
thoroughly good High School is a better guarantee
of fitness to take up college work than are the
examinations set by the very best of our American
Colleges and Universities. . . .   That official
evidence of having pursued such and such studies
for a specified time under competent teachers is the
best possible 'certificate of ripeness' for higher
work is the theory on which the Germans have long
proceeded; and surely the results achieved by their
system will compare very favourably with those
obtained in England and elsewhere by the system
of examinations."   The President, James B. Angell,
LL.D., one of the most eminent of American educators, stated in his address before Johns Hopkins
University, February, 1893, that in consequence of,
this custom, " the lifting and inspiring power of the
University is felt down through all the grades of
the most elementary class of the lowest schools.   It
is of vast consequence that teachers . . . should all
feel that their work is one; . . . such an alliance

imparts zest and pride to every teacher from the lowest to the highest, and strength and beauty to the whole educational system of a State."

So strong is the feeling against examinations that the students are not required to submit to any held by the University; the student has to attend lectures for fifteen hours a week for four years (or work that is reckoned equivalent). A card recording progress is kept. This is filled up regularly by the student, and countersigned by the professors and the University registrar. On this record the degree is given.

In the beginning of 1870, the privileges of the University were declared to be "the right of every resident of Michigan." In the autumn of that year, thirty-four women students entered; from that time to this the number has continually increased. The President informed the writer that there has never been the slightest difficulty in consequence of the adoption of the co-education system. No distinction is made in college discipline between men and women; they lodge with families in the town, or form clubs for co-operative residence. "Hundreds of women have availed themselves of the privileges offered them here, and have gone forth, several of them to foreign lands as missionary teachers or missionary physicians, many to various parts of our country as teachers in High Schools, academies and colleges, and the rest to those various duties, whether in professional careers, official positions, or in domestic life, which women of culture are fitted to discharge. The success of the experiment of admitting women to this institution was very influential in opening to them the doors of many colleges in this country, and was not without effect abroad." [1]   Several of these graduates did much in building up the women's Colleges which were established later.

The University is situated at Ann Arbor, a town on the main line of railway between Detroit and Chicago; its position makes it admirably suited for a centre of learning.   The country round is pleasant, and Ann Arbor itself is comparatively small, with no manufactures, and none of the distractions and temptations of a great city.   It is thus particularly suitable for a University where the students do not live in College.   The University buildings themselves stand on a large open space or campus, as it is termed, of forty acres, shaded with fine trees. Around, on all sides, extend streets of detached houses, many of them built of wood, all having gardens.   The most important building on the campus is University Hall, a very large and somewhat plain structure, devoted to lecture rooms and offices.   It contains an assembly hall, for more than 3,000 persons, with excellent acoustical properties. Around it are grouped the chemical, physical, and other laboratories, the law and medical schools, and the great library.   This latter differs from the

---

[1] We were told on excellent authority an interesting story of an elderly lady of means, who studied law at the University in order that she might devote herself to helping poor working women with professional advice a good work she carried on successfully for years after.

others in being elaborate and beautiful; the authorities, from the beginning, followed a principle enunciated early by one of its founders, that "men, not bricks and mortar, make a University." Nevertheless, although it can claim neither antiquity[1] nor beauty of architecture, the University of Michigan has that dignity and impressiveness which belongs to so large and important a seat of learning.

The library has over 80,000 volumes; its circular reading-room is fitted up for 210 readers; adjoining is an art gallery, containing casts from the antique, and fine specimens of the work of American sculptors. Besides the large reading-room, the library building contains smaller rooms for the work of advanced students, furnished with the books necessary for research—each room being devoted to a subject, English, History, Economics, etc. A gymnasium is being built, with a wing for the use of women students.

The social life of the University presents features of great interest; it is Western in the best sense.[2] "The whole policy of the administration of this University has been to make life here simple and inexpensive, and so a large proportion of our students have always supported themselves, in whole or in large part, by their own earnings. This has always been, and we are proud of the fact, the University of the poor."[3]

---

[1] "It is said that men now living have shot wild deer on the campus." [2] Chaps. cxiii. and civ. Bryce.
[3] President Angell's Oration.

In the course of our brief visit to Ann Arbor we formed a very favourable impression of its social life; members of the faculty take great interest in the students, although their official duties cease at the lecture room doors. The ladies of their families enter into friendly relations with the women students, so that something of the atmosphere of a family is formed. Through the kindness of the wife of the president we were introduced to one of the women students' clubs. Here a small number of girls lived together under the care of an older lady, chosen by themselves. Each girl had her own room, and the house contained also a reception room, where visitors of both sexes were received. Meals were obtained at one of the many boarding-houses in the town, this arrangement being considered more economical. Several of the Greek-letter fraternities [1] among the men students have also residential clubs, in buildings by the fraternities for the purpose. Some of these are of great architectural beauty. We visited that of the Ψ. Υ. The life here seemed to resemble that of an English College, with the difference that the students governed themselves, being responsible only to the officers of the fraternity.

The common social life of the students is largely aided by the University Students' Christian Association : this possesses a spacious and beautiful building adjacent to the University campus. Series of lectures are given here, and the building contains

---

[1] See Bryce, chap. ci. p. 562.

separate reading and sitting rooms for women. In connection with the churches of the city, guilds of students have been organized for religious and moral culture, and for social entertainment. Some of these have buildings and endowed lectureships for theology ; the University, as a State institution, is entirely undenominational.

In conclusion, we may remark that the University of Michigan, both on account of its peculiar characteristics, and the great work which it is doing for the higher education of the West, is, to an English observer, one of the most remarkable educational institutions in the United States.

CHAPTER VII

PHYSICAL EDUCATION

PHYSICAL education in American schools and colleges is a matter of comparatively recent development, and even now is not by any means as advanced as in England.[1] The reasons for this are easy to find. The earlier colonists, influenced as they were by a special type of Puritanism, and forced to consider the practical necessities of life by their environment, looked upon athletic exercises as a waste of time. In earlier days indeed, when towns were neither as large nor as numerous as now, the need for physical education was far less. Young people in the country found sufficient culture for their bodily powers in the work of the farm, during the seasons when no school was held, or in the wood-chopping and other semi-domestic duties throughout the year.[2] Many men too, then, as

---

[1] James Macalister. "Address on Physical Education."

[2] See Annual Address, University Convocation of the State of New York, 1891, by President Francis A. Walker. "These tasks . . . gave scope and play to the constructive faculty; they trained eye and hand to accuracy and precision. They taught the child to respect toil, and to value the fruits of labour. . . . To-day, under the new conditions of production, it would in almost every city, and in many village homes, cost more to keep a boy usefully employed than to

146

now, supported themselves during their College
career by actual manual labour; the writer met
several interesting cases of this custom, so honourable to the individual and so suggestive of the
mediæval Universities, and of Scottish student life.
In one the student acted as caretaker of a school,
tending the furnace and cleaning the floors in the
daily intervals of college work. Such men have
neither time nor energy for the athletic sports of
our English Universities.

Several causes have, however, contributed to
arouse American educators to the need for
systematic physical training in modern times.
Two of these are historical: first the influx of
German immigrants, bringing with them their
Turnvereine, and their masculine vigour and enthusiasm for gymnastics; and second, the War—the
civil war of 1861-65—which has brought about so
many changes.[1] Neither of these causes would,
however, directly affect the education of girls; we
need not, therefore, discuss them at length, noting
only that the German influence came to affect girls
and women ultimately, and that the regular military
drill, introduced into colleges and schools for male
students, and often forming part-of the curriculum
—as in the Universities of Minnesota and Illinois—
has been adopted in some excellent private schools
for girls as inducing a good carriage.[2] We did not

feed him in idleness. Even play of any satisfactory sort is
scarcely practicable in our modern cities."

[1] Bureau of Education Circular on Physical Training.

[2] Ogontz. Pa., and Lasell Seminary, Mass.

meet with it in any of the public High Schools for
girls, although it seemed to be the rule for boys.
The weightiest reason, however, for the attention
paid to physical education for girls in the present
day is the change in the ways of living, consequent
upon the growth of towns and of wealth, which has
brought about a condition of high nervous tension,
injurious to both sexes, but especially affecting
women.   This condition is matter of common
comment in the United States.   We frequently
heard Americans refer to the good health of English
women, and to their delight in open-air games,
while they regretted that such customs did not
prevail more generally in America.   The women's
Colleges have led the way in organizing physical
training for women, and their influence in this
respect is likely to increase.

We must, however, return to the historical aspect
of the question.   Under the influence of the German
societies, the Colleges for men took up the matter
about 1850, and in 1860 several college gymnasia
were built.   In 1879 a great impulse was given to
the cause by the opening of the Hemenway Gymnasium at Harvard, and by the appointment of Dr.
Sargent, of the Yale Medical School, as Assistant
Professor of Physical Training, and Director of the
Gymnasium.   His system has great influence in the
United States, and many of the women teachers of
physical culture have been trained by him.   He has
a special gymnasium in Cambridge for women, which
the students of Harvard Annex attend.

The essential feature of the Sargent system is the

physical examination of each student, and the prescription for him of exercises specially intended to correct his defects. The chief means for these exercises is furnished by Dr. Sargent's appliances, each of which is adapted for strengthening a particular portion of the body, so that a man can gradually be prepared for using the ordinary heavy apparatus. Free exercises, and movements with dumb-bells, wands, clubs, etc., also form part of the system, which is often spoken of as though synonymous with the German method. The measurements taken at the physical examination of the individual are carefully recorded, and comparison made, by periodic re-examination, of the effect of the exercises. It appears that there is in America a very close relation between the medical profession and physical education. Medical women are in charge of this department in all the chief women's Colleges.

In 1884, Dr. Sargent opened a school for training teachers in Cambridge; summer courses for teachers are also held. In Dr. Hopkins' Report on Physical Education previously referred to, is a list of forty-eight important institutions which have adopted Dr. Sargent's system.[1] Further details on the cost of gymnasia, plan and elevation of buildings, etc., are given in the same work, to which reference should be made by any who may desire fuller information.

In connection with the anthropological measurements of the students in American Colleges, an interesting artistic exhibit was shown at the World's

---

[1] "Bureau of Education Circular."

Fair. Two statues, one male and one female, have
been made from the actual average measurements
taken by Dr. Sargent at Harvard, and by the
teachers at the Annex and the women's Colleges.
When we visited Chicago the anthropological
building was not yet opened, but by the courtesy of
the author we obtained the proofs of an article by
an eminent American litterateur,[1] from which this
account is taken. The girl's figure is said to be
typically feminine; the sculptor thinks it nearer
the Greek ideal than the man's; it will probably
not suffer in comparison with that of the girl who
has not had a college education, although, as there
are no measurements for *her*, the comparison is not
easy to make. " The essential point is that it is
fairly healthful, fairly attractive, and, above all,
thoroughly womanly. . . . This being the case,
nature and the gymnastic teachers will provide for
all the rest."

The Swedish System has been recently introduced
into the United States, and is being taken up vigorously in some quarters. In Boston, a Normal School
of Gymnastics was established in 1893, by Mrs.
Hemenway, to give thorough instruction in the
Swedish system to women and men who desire to
conduct gymnasia, or otherwise to teach.[2] It has a
thoroughly qualified staff, 14 in number, including
some of the Harvard professors, who lecture in science.
Its students, after a two years' course, receive a

---

[1] Colonel T. W. Higginson, of Cambridge.
[2] Catalogue, 1893, Amy M. Homans, Director.

diploma; this course includes biology, anatomy, physiology, and emergency lectures, as well as pedagogy. Some educators, however, feel that the physique of American young people is so different from that of Swedes, that the system will require modification for use in America. It demands too much intense concentration to be suitable for the nervous condition of American city children.[1]

A third system of physical culture has influenced physical education in the United States; this is known by the title Delsartianized Physical Culture. Delsarte, himself, had nothing to do with physical training in schools; he was an actor and teacher of elocution, and his system was one intended to teach the proper mode of expression by gesture, for the use of actors, public speakers, and others; it thus has affinities with art, especially with the art of dancing, rather than with education. It has been studied, however, by American teachers of physical culture, its principles to some extent adopted, and its practice mingled with that of other systems. Thus has arisen an eclectic system which aims at the culture of grace and repose, and is especially suited to girls, its exponents claiming that it counteracts that nervous tension which is at present so prevalent among American women. Its objects are health, strength, agility, flexibility, grace, and control.

On several occasions [2] the writer witnessed some

---

[1] Dr. Luther Gullick, of Springfield, Mass., at the University Convocation, State of New York, 1891.

[2] Girls' High School, Baltimore; Mount Vernon Seminary, Washington; Normal College, New York.

excellent work in this method; it was, indeed, the
excellence of the work done by the pupils, and the
grace and skill of the teachers, that first directed our
attention to the system. It deserves the careful
study of English teachers, as it seems to contain
features which appeal to girls, arousing their interest, and so inducing them to work more heartily.
Unfortunately, Delsarte's name has been associated
with much mystical and æsthetic vapouring, and
scientific educators have thus been led to look
down upon it; Delsarte's system also lends itself
easily to ridicule as a fashionable craze. But it is
certainly successful in the schoolroom, when modi-
fied and adapted by an able teacher. Two principles contained in it are of particular importance,
the principle of rhythmic movement and the
principle of relaxation; the latter is especially concerned with conditions of nervous strain, the culture
of power through repose having, it is said, a
strengthening effect upon the nerves. Teachers say,
however, that the German and Swedish systems are
also required for complete development. "From
the Delsarte system we get the relaxing exercises
which make the muscles flexible, give ease of
movement, prepare the body for gesture. From the
German system we get energizing or strength-
giving exercises, requiring more vigorous muscular
action."

Vassar.

This College enjoys the advantage of spacious
grounds; special arrangements being made for lawn
tennis, fifteen courts are provided by the College.

The asphalt and gravel walks, several miles in extent, furnish good roads for cycling, and many students follow this form of exercise. A small lake is available for boating and skating, and there is a fine rink (100 feet by 40 feet) for ice skating—the gift of one of the trustees, Mr. Rockefeller—which can be flooded in the winter. The alumnæ (old students) have recently erected a large and well-appointed gymnasium, the upper storey of which is used as a tennis court and as a hall for dramatic entertainments. Below is a swimming tank, 43 feet by 24 feet, as well as dressing rooms and baths.

The Sargent system is followed, the prescribed exercises being required three times a week. Careful measurements are taken periodically, and, as elsewhere, these show clearly the valuable effects of systematic physical training. The annual prospectus declares " students, who enter in good health, have almost uniformly preserved it." Students are expected to take daily exercise in some form or other, and to retire to rest at 10 p.m. The opinion of the president, which, of course, carries great weight, is that the women's colleges in America have helped to raise the standard of health among women.

Wellesley.

We quote from the Calendar as follows : —

" The physicians with the director of the gymnasium, the physical examiner, and the professor of elocution constitute a Board of Health, under whose direction the students are examined on admission to the College. . . . From the records of these examinations the exercises in the gymnasium are adapted to meet the special wants of each student. The gymnasium is equipped with the Swedish apparatus and with Dr. Sargent's machines."

The Swedish system has been recently introduced, but only for the Freshmen year, as the limited space available in the gymnasium does not allow the attendance of all the 700 students. Regular lessons are given three times a week, and are compulsory, the resident physician, of course, allowing special exemptions. The students are carefully measured during the course, and are found to improve considerably. The lessons are said to be popular and successful, and the second year students regret that they cannot go on with the Swedish exercises; in the upper classes physical training is elective.

Doubtless, Wellesley will soon have an adequately equipped gymnasium erected from that reservoir of wealth which, in America, seems always available for educational purposes. The formal training is, however, relatively less important here, because of the truly magnificent resources which the College possesses in the extensive grounds and the beautiful lake. Boating is regularly organized, the Oxford stroke being carefully taught under a competent coach.[1] One cannot soon forget the charming picture presented on a spring evening at Wellesley, when the water is alive with parties of happy young girls, and the surrounding quiet makes their voices sound the merrier. There are thirteen courts for lawn

---

[1] Practice with rowing machines goes on during the winter, and the crews (40 in number) are selected from those of the 150 girls practising who do best.

tennis. The extent, solitude, and the beauty of the grounds should encourage walking, but the large demands made on the time of the students, by the number of College lectures they have to attend, prevent them taking that degree of physical exercise which is possible under our more elastic University system. It is to be hoped that, at some future time, the golf and hockey of Girton College, and the cricket of St. Leonard's School, Fife, may be introduced in a College where the natural surroundings are so well fitted for games.

All students in the College buildings aid in the lighter domestic work, or in clerical labour,—the time given being about 45 minutes daily. The aim of this regulation is to promote moral training and habits of respect for labour. But the sweeping, laying tables, etc., are certainly forms of physical exercise. The general health of the students is remarkably good, only 29 out of the 700 withdrawing during the year on account of physical debility.[1] The investigation of the physical examiner in the gymnasium points to two causes for what is to English ideas a large percentage,—over pressure in preparation for College and the work in vacation, either to supplement inadequate preparation, or to earn money.

Smith College.

This, like the other Colleges, has a resident physician, who controls the physical training ; a specialist examines each student and prescribes for

---

[1] President's Report, Wellesley College.

her particular exercises. There are also regular class exercises in light gymnastics, the Swedish system being used, but very carefully lest there be over-strain.

There is an excellent gymnasium, the gift of the alumnæ, with baths and a swimming tank. Gymnastics do not rank as a study, but the first and second years are required to give four half-hours per week to gymnastic practice.[1]

Tennis courts are numerous, and the picturesque mountainous country around affords interesting walks. The rule of retiring to rest at 10 p.m. is considered very important, and is carefully observed.

Bryn Mawr College.

This College possesses an admirable gymnasium, said to be one of the best in the United States, equipped with all Dr. Sargent's apparatus, and under the charge of a director who has completed his course of instruction. The building, which is a type of the best gymnasiums in women's Colleges and girls' schools, contains a large hall for gymnastic exercises, with a running or walking track for use in rainy weather, a room for the director, another for examination and record of the physical development of the students, and bath-rooms for use after exercise. It is open at all times to the students, and they are required before graduation to give a certain number of hours to practice there. Before admission each student is examined, and a course of

---

[1] "Gymnastic Work at Smith College." Miss E. C. Laurence, University Convocation, State of New York, 1891.

exercises suited to her individual needs is laid down for her; the effect of these is tested by half-yearly medical examinations. At the time of our visit students were practising with apparent pleasure and thoroughness on the various Sargent machines, or on the more familiar ropes, bars, etc., of an English gymnasium. A woman physician from Philadelphia visits the College every week, and can be consulted by the students free of charge. There are lawn-tennis courts in the grounds, but they seem to belong primarily to the faculty, who are chiefly men resident in the neighbourhood. It would seem that free games for the women students are somewhat alien to the austere spirit of Bryn Mawr, and that formal prescribed work in the gymnasium is considered sufficient.

Physical Training in the Public Schools.

The movement here is not as far advanced as in the colleges, but progress is being made. The most usual custom is for the Board of a city to employ a specialist teacher of physical culture, who gives lessons to the ordinary teachers; they in turn taking their own classes, for a few minutes at a time every day. The specialist teacher also gives each class an occasional lesson, and inspects the work. We saw some work of a very simple character, done with very small children, in the Washington schools; the children stood at their desks and went through the exercise at the word of command. In the exhibit at Chicago, in the Washington State Building, were elaborate photographs of a display by the children of the grammar school at Seattle, Washington, where the teacher is a woman. These exercises were similar to those in use in England.

In the High Schools as a rule the boys have military drill, the girls have calisthenics. Too often, however, the lesson is given only once a week, and is therefore, we should consider, of but little value. We were present at several such lessons; the girls seemed interested, and the teaching was excellent, except in one case, where a man gave the lesson to a mixed class of boys and girls. No public High School that we visited had a regular gymnasium with apparatus; several private schools however had excellent and well-fitted gymnasia.

We did not meet with any case of a special costume being required for physical exercises in the public schools, probably because the exercises are of so simple a character; for public displays a fancy dress is worn, but that applies to a few girls only. When a gymnasium dress is worn, as in the Colleges, it consists invariably of a blouse and knickerbockers so full that a skirt is not required. Some teachers indeed positively object to the skirt, as likely to catch in apparatus and cause accidents. Some of the best private schools forbid the corset altogether, not only for physical exercise, but at all times in school. This is easier to enforce than in England, as many varieties of bodices (termed waists) are sold in America as substitutes for the corset. When military drill is given in a girls' private school, the girls are required to be provided with a military cap and belt, a small wooden musket, and simple blouse and skirt.

Vocal music is taught regularly in the common schools of most cities; we were surprised to find how rarely the Tonic Sol-fa system was employed; many teachers were wholly ignorant of it. In many High Schools one lesson a week is given in class singing; we heard several such lessons, the teacher being in every case a man. The work was very similar to what is done in England; there was perhaps less fulness and richness of tone than might have been expected from the numbers. The songs sung were more classic in character than in most English schools; the text-books, as in other subjects, were superior. We heard some especially beautiful singing in the Coloured High School in Washington.

Very much more attention is paid to Elocution in American schools and colleges than with us; we did not notice any superiority in the manner of reading or answering over what is heard in England; the same faults are common to the pupils of both countries. Teachers seem to lay most stress on realizing the inner meaning of a passage to be recited ; we were, however, not able to give much time to this subject.

It is clear from what has been said above that great attention is now being paid to physical education in America; the subject is discussed frequently at teachers' meetings, in reports of superintendents, and elsewhere. To an English critic, however, the comparative absence of free games is a serious fault. No formal method can do as much for physical health and development as games in the open air, pursued freely and not as a task. We do not refer to boys in this criticism; athletics at men's colleges and in boys' schools were outside the scope of the present inquiry; but we feel obliged to say that games are not encouraged in the women's colleges and girls' schools as they are in England. The difference of national habit must of course be allowed for; climate too is a factor, but when so much is being done for gymnastic training, it seems strange that more effort is not given to the introduction and organization of games suitable for women and girls in institutions for secondary and higher education.

CHAPTER VIII

CO-EDUCATION OF BOYS AND GIRLS

CO-EDUCATION is almost everywhere the custom in American public elementary schools. The common school of the rural districts has always been a mixed school, like the old parish schools of Scotland, and for the same reason. The city schools followed this example. In the public High Schools, however, there is occasionally a difference, the girls having a separate school, although co-education prevails in the elementary schools of the place. Boston is an example of this peculiarity; but the reason is not to be found in any pedagogic theory, but in the fact that originally there was *no* public secondary education for girls, and that when public opinion demanded that High Schools should be open to them, it was more convenient to provide a separate school. The Boston Boys' Latin School is 250 years old; the Girls' Latin School dates only from 1852.

There are ten High Schools under the Boston School Board, four separate and six co-educational. The latter belong to the suburbs, which were originally small towns, and which have now been incorporated in Boston. No alteration has been made in these, so clearly the existence of separate

Girls' High Schools in Boston is not to be taken to mean that Boston educational opinion does not favour co-education.   At Cambridge, and Brookline, near Boston, the High Schools are co-educational, as the writer learnt from visiting them.   The same obtains, we believe, in New England generally.   In Brooklyn, New York, and Philadelphia, there is one great Girls' High School, called in the two last named cities a Normal College.   The Brooklyn High School for girls was founded at a later date than that for boys, so it seems analogous to that of Boston.   Baltimore has separate High Schools for girls; Washington on the other hand has not.   There are four High Schools in that city, all co-educational, three for pupils of white race, and one for the coloured people.   In the West co-education is universal, both in elementary and High Schools.

These observations refer, of course, only to public schools; as far as we could learn, no private schools adopt co-education.

Full details on this subject are to be found in one of the Circulars of the Bureau of Education, "Co-education of the Sexes in the Public Schools of the United States."[1]   This pamphlet gives the reasons for co-education, as stated by teachers and super-intendents.   They may be formulated as follows:—

"Co-education of the sexes is preferred because it is *Natural*, following the ordinary structure of the family and of society; *Customary*, being in harmony with the habits and sentiments of everyday life, and of the laws of the State; *Impartial*, affording one sex the same opportunity for

---

[1] Teachers' Guild Library.

culture that the other enjoys; *Economical,* using the school funds to the best advantage; *Convenient,* both for superintendents and teachers, in assigning grading, teaching, and discipline; *Beneficial,* to the minds, morals, habits, and development of the pupils."

We have quoted the passage in full, as it states so concisely the various advantages claimed for co-education. We were not able to learn much on the subject from interviews or from personal observation. The custom was so natural, and so harmonious with the social usages of American life,[1] that there seemed to be little to say. The one fact we learnt from conversation with teachers was that co-education made discipline *easier.* This seemed to be a generally accepted truism. The boys are restrained by the presence of the girls, and the latter are roused and stimulated to study by the example of the boys. We repeatedly asked whether teachers found any difference of method necessary in addressing either sex, or whether the rates of development were different, but the answer was always in the negative. In fact teachers who had experience in co-educational schools always declared themselves to be perfectly satisfied with the system, and to find no difficulties in it. We might perhaps note here that there is generally a Lady Vice-Principal of a mixed High School who is specially responsible for the girls, and whom they can consult on matters of health. In the class-room no difference was to be observed between boys and girls; they sat where they pleased, and their conduct and answering were

---

[1] Bryce, chap. civ. p. 600.

of the same quality, but out of class there seemed to be very little general intercourse,—girls speaking to girls, and boys to boys.   At recess the sexes are generally separated, the boys occupying the basement, and the girls the upper part of the buildings.

We were unable to obtain any information as to the conditions, if any, under which co-education becomes unsuccessful.   A teacher of experience, a principal of a large public High School, gave to the writer an interesting comparison between boys and girls.   When the girls enter the High School, they are more mature, more honest in work, with greater power of concentration, and are more apt in acquiring information.   This lasts for a year or two; then the boys develop, and become at 16 thinking beings. At 18 years of age the girls' work in general becomes worthless, other interests claiming their attention. Boys excel in mathematics, economics, and civics; girls hold their own in languages and history, and many do well in science.   Girls always do *rote* work better than their brothers.

When we come to the University the question of co-education assumes an entirely different aspect in America; whether students of both sexes, of the college age, should be educated together in the lecture room and laboratory is, even at the present day, the subject of warm discussion, and one on which prominent educators hold utterly diverse opinions.

This seems specially strange when co-education in the schools has been the custom for many years. The subject was discussed at the University Convocation of the State of New York, in July, 1891. Some extracts from the record of the proceedings will perhaps give the varying arguments from the American standpoint.

President Taylor, of Vassar, declares :—[1]

"Without any question, it seems to me that there is more danger that in a co-educational College there will be a certain loss of influence that is needed about the life of almost every young girl to encourage the more refined feelings and tendencies of life, and a greater temptation, than can possibly exist in the separate College. . . . There is a feeling in my own mind that in these years of College life there is a certain tranquillity that enters into the life that is separated from its general social conditions; a certain restfulness that comes to both boy and girl in just that separation, and a certain lack of restfulness that comes to both boy and girl in the other relations. *And I believe that it is of immense value in this American life of ours, if we can give such a period of tranquillity, by this means, to both boy and girl.*"

On the other hand, the upholders of co-education, such as Ex-President White, of Cornell, declared at the same meeting that co-education in Universities had been successful in practice, and that evil results had not followed. A Boston lady, Miss Alla W. Foster, asserted, "Co-education is an unqualified success at Michigan and at Boston University." The writer visited the University of Michigan at Ann Arbor, as described in a previous chapter, where some account is given of the social life of the students. From all we could gather in that institution, there have been no difficulties, although the students do not live in dormitories (College halls), but are free to reside where they like. We

---

[1] Regent's Bulletin, 1893, pp. 426-7.

were informed that after graduation, students not unfrequently marry; but this is not considered as a drawback, but rather as an advantage to the system. All the Western State Universities are co-educational, and so is the new University of Chicago. At the latter, however, there are to be special halls of residence for women, with a responsible Lady Principal; social life here will probably be modelled somewhat on the Eastern type. In the article dealing with the Harvard Annex (page 118) reference has been made to the feeling at Cambridge (Mass.) against women students attending lectures with the men, but we were unable to ascertain the reasons for this.

CHAPTER IX

IT may perhaps be advisable to select from the main body of the Report those features of the American educational system which seem to the writer most worthy of study by English educators.

Whatever may be the differences between England and America in regard to local government, one conclusion at least may be drawn from the phenomena of the American public school system. It is *that the combination of local and central* authorities is absolutely necessary. The best proof of this is found in the Massachusetts system; the formation of the High School Board of Minnesota, the revival of the University of the State of New York, illustrate it. It may be noted that the powers of the Central Boards are advisory and supervisory rather than compulsory; the influence of these bodies on secondary education in particular has been excellent.[1] The Central State Boards generally have been established in order to make up for the deficiencies of local bodies, and many American teachers desire that the powers of these central authorities should be increased. The reason for this is the evil influence

---

[1] See Bureau of Education Report, 1889–90.

of politics in local government. The corruption of municipal life in America is, however, due so entirely to Transatlantic conditions of foreign immigration, the spoils system, etc., etc., that no inference can fairly be drawn from American experience in this matter: we can only say that political influence *does* seriously injure the public schools in the United States, especially in the great cities; we cannot say that the same evil would occur in England, for our political life is entirely different.

Another conclusion may perhaps be drawn safely: it is that *small areas ad hoc* are bad in the organization of a public school system. The area should be the same as for other purposes of local government, and should be moderately large.

American systems throw little light on the vexed question as to whether Boards should be elected for educational purposes only, or whether Town and County Councils should control education also. It can only be said that the former is almost universally the case. In Buffalo, where the schools are said to be very bad,[1] the Town Council governs them, but this is an isolated instance. Some of the best Central Boards are those in which *teachers* are represented, as for instance the Indiana Board, and the High School Board of Minnesota. No conclusions can be drawn as to the relative merits of the methods of popular election and nomination in the formation of educational committees: the Massachusetts State Board, which is excellent, is

---

[1] Dr. Rice, in *The Forum*.

nominated by the Governor; the Regents of the University of Michigan, a body high in public esteem, is elected by the people at the polls; there are examples of inefficient and even corrupt Boards, both elective and nominated.

The influence of the professional teacher is exercised chiefly by the method we have now to discuss, the Superintendent system.

There is nothing corresponding to this, we believe, in England, though the organising secretaries and advisers for technical education appointed by some of the County Councils approximate to the type; its great merit is that the skill of an expert is brought to the aid of local bodies in the management of schools, while, as each town or district has its own Superintendent, the danger of the rigid uniformity of excessive centralization is avoided. It might be thought that teachers would find their freedom in teaching restrained by the action of the Superintendent in laying down courses of study, etc. We questioned many teachers, especially those who are not *now* teaching in the public schools, whether they felt this; they all replied in the negative. It appears that a really able teacher of high attainments is left to herself, and indeed is often consulted by the Superintendent on her own subject. His work is rather to deal with the inexperienced teachers, and to co-ordinate all the schools. The principal of a High School, although technically answerable to the Superintendent, seems in practice to have almost entire control of his own school. We met with one case in which the principal had previously been a Superintendent in the same city.

The third point is that of discipline, which has been treated at some length in Chapter II. It is our deliberate opinion that America has advanced beyond England in this respect. The American pupil has also far more self-reliance, and is trained to depend on himself from the beginning. The principles of Pestalozzi and Froebel appear in action there, not only in the Kindergarten, but throughout the whole educational system. Love of knowledge is the determining motive. Prizes and competitive examinations are rare, especially in the best schools. It must, of course, be remembered that differences in national and social characteristics have great influence in this matter, and it may therefore not be possible for English teachers to follow American methods entirely at present.

It is impossible to state positively whether the America "recitation" method described in Chapter IV. is, even at its best, preferable to those in use in England. It is certain, however, that many English teachers are not as skilful as those of America in making pupils work for themselves. The question of the use of good, and therefore expensive, text-books, and of school libraries, is however involved in this, as is also that of preparing for examinations. Probably each country has much to learn from the other in the technique of teaching.

The American custom of having a lesson studied on each subject every day, might well be followed in England; it saves time and energy, and pupils make greater progress than when their minds are diverted by studying many subjects at once.

In Chapter IV., in dealing with the teaching of history, we alluded to the work which is done in American schools to develop an intelligent and earnest patriotism in the children. England has much to learn from America in this respect. The difficulties there are at least as great as in England; party spirit runs high, the people are homogeneous neither in race nor in religion, and burning questions such as were involved in the war of North and South are not wanting. Nevertheless, teachers deal with the institutions and present history of the nation, and impart to their pupils an intelligent, and at the same time earnest, enthusiasm for their country. We have alluded to the influence of the national holidays, especially Washington's birthday, and Memorial Day, and to the patriotic exercises held in schools in connection with these. The use of the national flag in schoolhouses might easily be adopted in England. For this purpose many schools are provided with flags, which are displayed upon festal or public occasions. The back of the platform of a school assembly hall is often decorated with the national colours as a symbol of the common feeling of loyalty which unites all members of the school, however much they may differ in other respects.

The Research system in the Colleges and Universities, which is referred to more especially in Chapter V. (Bryn Mawr College) is worthy of careful attention by those interested in collegiate instruction for women. It is certainly true that much of the post-graduate work in American Colleges corresponds in standard to that done in preparation for an Honour Degree at Oxford and Cambridge, but the method is different, the students being taught how to do research, and not being required to consider what is demanded by the examiners. It seems somewhat anomalous that former women students of English Colleges should be following advanced courses of study in America, under English teachers,[1] because they were unable to find opportunities of doing so at home.

The system of fellowships at Bryn Mawr has an important influence on the question of post-graduate work. The Association of College Alumnæ, a body of college women, also grants two fellowships for the encouragement of research. The new University of Chicago has established a large number of fellowships open to both men and women. It is probable that a well qualified Englishwoman might be able to obtain one of these in order to study a year at Chicago. Yale is also open to women who desire to do post-graduate work, and so is the University of Pennsylvania, Philadelphia. The objections to co-education felt so keenly at the great Eastern Universities are held to be inapplicable to the case of older and more advanced students. We understand that even at Johns Hopkins, Baltimore, a highly qualified woman might be admitted in this department by special permission. The facilities

---

[1] This was the case at Bryn Mawr during the Session 1892–1893.

for research there are, as well known, exceptionally
good, particularly in history and political science.

It is no part of our work to criticize American
schools, and point out where the adoption of
English methods might be of advantage. Such a
judgment from a stranger might be presumptuous,
and would certainly be uncalled for in this relation.
The whole subject is one of extreme difficulty,
especially when national differences have to be
taken into account. There are, however, two points
on which some comment might be made, as they
concern general pedagogic questions. The first is,
that sufficient effort is not given in the public
secondary schools of America to develope the
individual talents of a particular boy or girl. All
are treated in sections and sets, and are made to
advance together along the specified lines of an
arbitrary course; no provision seems to have been
made for enabling pupils to develope along their own
lines at varying rates. To do this means a large
staff of the most highly educated men and women,
who are also good teachers, and are inspired with
zeal for knowledge, and for humanity. Nevertheless America, with all her wealth, could surely
afford such teachers in her public schools. It would
be better to spend less on buildings and apparatus,
and more on salaries, to secure this end. A country
which provides only for the average youth in its
public schools deprives the boy or girl who possesses
special talents of the opportunity of cultivating
them to the highest possible degree, and thus robs
itself. As America demands, and rightly, the most

perfect products of the Old World for æsthetic and social enjoyment, she ought to be satisfied with nothing short of perfection in the realms of intellectual life. This is costly and difficult of attainment, like the technique of an art : how difficult and how costly public opinion in America as yet hardly recognizes. To form such an ideal, to make the average man realize it, is probably one of the most urgent tasks of the present day for American specialists in higher education.

Our second criticism has been made already ; it refers to the women's Colleges, to their long hours of work, and to the apparent absence of repose and opportunity for thought and individual development consequent upon such excessive demands on the students' time. We can add nothing to what has been said already—we can only reiterate it. Probably this defect, like the former, is ultimately due to one cause, which we have attempted to explain in the previous paragraph. To try to do too much in a given time often comes from an incorrect idea of the labour necessary to finish one thing perfectly. It is only natural that in a country where the industrial conquest of a continent, elsewhere the work of two thousand years, has been achieved in two generations, the average man should consider that the intellectual kingdom is also to be taken by violence. The American scholar knows already the arduousness of the task ; Germany has taught him ; as yet he has not often sought his scholarship in England ; in time the average man will learn the truth also.

Here, as in other questions, the best hope for the future is that the two great nations of the English-speaking race may come to know one another better. Each has something to give the other; their commerce should be not only in wheat and in textiles, in cotton and in steel, but in the weightier matters of knowledge and truth.

To aid such a consummation is, we conceive, the purpose of the Gilchrist Educational Trust in sending their travelling scholars to America. To have been privileged to take a part, however small, in the attainment of such an end is, to the writer of this report, not only an honour, but a joy.

LIST OF INSTITUTIONS VISITED.
1893.

State.	City.	Number.	Institution.	Whether co-educational.	Remarks.
District of Columbia.	Washington.	1	Franklin School.	Yes.	Public elementary school for white children.
		2	Polk School.	Yes.	
		3	Henry School.	Yes.	
		4	Sumner School.	Yes.	Public elementary school for coloured children.
		5	Macgruder School.	Yes.	
		6	Cooking School.	No.	For girls of public schools.
		7	Workshop School.	No.	For boys of public schools.
		8	Central High School.	Yes.	For white pupils.
		9	Coloured High School.	Yes.	For coloured pupils.
		10	Mount Vernon Seminary.	No.	Private school.
		11	Norwood Institute.	No.	Private school.
		12	Catholic University.	No.	For priests only. Magnificent building; fine laboratories.
		13	Howard University.	Yes.	Chiefly for coloured people.
		14	Bureau of Education.		United States National Institution. See chap. I.
		15	Smithsonian Institute.		
		16	Calvary Baptist Sunday School.	No.	Over 1,000 members, including adults.

State.	City.	Number.	Institution.	Whether co-edu-cational.	Remarks.
District of Co-lunbia.	Washington.	17	Wesley Chapel Sunday School.	No.	Large numbers, adults included.
Illinois.	Chicago.	18	Chautauqua Circle.	Yes.	Home Reading Union.
		19	Hyde Park High School.	Yes.	
		20	Cook County Normal School.	Yes.	
		21	Elementary School.	Yes.	Practising School for the Normal School.
		22	University of Chicago.	Yes.	See chapter v.
Maryland	Baltimore.	23	Girls' Western High School.	No.	An old building.
		24	Women's College of Baltimore.	No.	Magnificent buildings ; belongs to Methodist Episcopal Church.
		25	Girls' Latin School.	No.	Connected with the Women's College.
		26	Bryn Mawr School.	No.	Magnificent building; resembles an English High School.

N

State.	City.	Number.	Institution.	Whether co-educational.	Remarks.
Maryland.	Baltimore.	27	Johns Hopkins University.	No.	The great University of the Middle States.
Massachusetts.	Boston.	28	Girls' Latin School.	No.	Among the best and most famous public schools for girls in the United States.
		29	Girls' High School.	No.	,, ,, ,,
		30	Massachusetts Institute of Technology.	Yes.	A great scientific University resembling the Zurich Polytechnic.
		31	State Board of Education Office.	No.	See chapter I. section B.
		32	College Club.	No.	For College women; chiefly social functions.
		33	Women's Educational and Industrial Union.	No.	For working women of all classes.
	Brookline.	34	Lincoln School.	Yes.	Public elementary schools. Work excellent.
		35	Pierce School.	Yes.	
		36	Laurence School.	Yes.	
		37	Kindergarten School.	Yes.	
		38	High School.	Yes.	Prepares largely for College.

State.	City.	Number.	Institution.	Whether co-educational.	Remarks.
Massachusetts.	Cambridge.	39	Latin School.	Yes.	Excellent schools, preparing largely for college. Buildings extremely well designed.
		40	High School.	Yes.	
		41	Mr. Gilman's School.	No.	Private school connected with the Annex; prepares for college.
		42	Margaret Winthrop Hall.	No.	Residence for girls attending above school.
		43	The Harvard Annex.	No.	Women's College; see chap. v.
		44	Harvard College, including Library.	No.	The Oxford or Cambridge of America.
		45		Yes.	Open to students of the Annex.
		46	Agassiz Museum.	Yes.	Open to students of natural history.
		47	Peabody Museum.	Yes.	Open to students of ethnology.
		48	Hemingway Gymnasium.	No.	The home of the Sargent System. See chap. vii.
	Northampton.	49	Smith College.	No.	See chap. v.

State.	City.	Number.	Institution.	Whether co-educational.	Remarks.
Massachusetts.	Wellesley.	50	Dana Hall.	No.	Private school preparing for college.
		51	Wellesley College.	No.	See chap. v.
Michigan.	Ann Arbor.	52	High School.	Yes.	See chap. vi.
		53	University of Michigan.	Yes.	A very large and well-organized public school.
New York.	Brooklyn.	54	Girls' High School.	No.	
		55	Pratt Institute.	Yes.	A famous technical institute privately endowed.
		56	Pratt Institute High School.	Yes.	In connection with the Institute.
	New York.	57	College of the City of New York.	No.	Public high school for boys.
		58	Normal College.	No.	Training college and public high school for girls; has an academic department.
		59	Brearley School.	No.	Admirable and well-equipped private schools; magnificent buildings.
		60	Dr. Sachs' School.	No.	
		61	College for Training Teachers.	Yes.	Special attention paid to science and manual work.

State.	City.	Number.	Institution.	Whether co-educational.	Remarks.
New York.	New York.	62	Barnard College.	No.	The Annex of Columbia College. Its students obtain the Columbia degrees.
	Poughkeepsie.	63	Vassar College.	No.	The oldest women's college. See chap. v.
Pennsylvania.	Philadelphia.	64	Girls' Normal College.	No.	Public high school; very large.
		65	Friends' Central High School.	No.	} Private schools preparing for college.
		66	Miss Case's School.	No.	
		67	Ogontz.	No.	Private boarding school.
		68	Drexel Institute.	Yes.	Privately endowed technical institute; magnificent building.
		69	Miss Stuart's Kindergarten Training College.		Private.
		70	Swarthmore College.	Yes.	Belongs to the Society of Friends.
		71	Bryn Mawr College.	No.	The equivalent of Johns Hopkins for women.
		72	Univ. of Pennsylvania.	No.	Colonial foundation; magnificent building; great medical school.

181

In the *educational exhibit at the World's Fair*, a special study was made of the following States and institutions (the order represents roughly the degree of attention given to each):—Massachusetts, Minnesota, California, Illinois, Washington (Seattle Exhibition), Pennsylvania, Hampton (Va), Ohio (especially Cincinnati and Cleveland), Colorado, Indiana, Iowa, Nebraska, Kansas, West Virginia, and Florida.

BIBLIOGRAPHY.

I.

WORKS DEALING WITH THE SUBJECT GENERALLY.

R. G. BOONE: Education in the United States. (International Education Series, New York, 1890.)

J. BRYCE: The American Commonwealth. (2nd Edition, London, 1889.)

F. BUISSON: Rapport sur l'Instruction primaire aux Etats Unis. (Paris, 1878.)

J. G. FITCH: Notes on American Schools and Training Colleges. (London, 1890.)
Memorandum on the Working of the Free School System in America. (Education Department, London, 1891.)

S. JEX-BLAKE: A Visit to some American Schools and Colleges. (London, 1867.)

MARIE LOIZILLON: Rapport sur l'Education des Enfants aux Etats Unis. (Paris, 1883.)

J. RICE: *Forum*, for October, 1892, to June, 1893. Articles on American Education. (New York.)

II.

REPORTS AND CIRCULARS OF PUBLIC BODIES AND INSTITUTIONS ARRANGED BY STATES AND CITIES.

Bureau of Education.

1. Reports of the Commissioner of Education.
   For 1888–1889. 2 vols. (Washington, 1891.)
   „ 1889–1890. 2 vols. („ 1893.)
2. Circulars of Information of the Bureau.

H. B. ADAMS: The Study of History in American Schools and Colleges. (Washington, 1887.)

F. W. BLACKMAR: Federal and State Aid to Higher Education in the United States. (Washington, 1890.)

FLORIAN CAJORI: Teaching and History of Mathematics in the U.S. (Wash., 1890.)

J. P. CAMPBELL: Biological Teaching in the Colleges of the United States. (Wash., 1891.)

E. M. HARTWELL, M.D.: Physical Training in American Schools and Colleges. (Wash., 1886.)

A. MCLAUGHLIN: History of Higher Education in Michigan. (Wash., 1891.)

J. D. PHILBRICK: City School Systems of the U.S.A. (Wash., 1885.)

C. H. WEAD: Aims and Methods of the Teaching of Physics. (Wash., 1884.)

Co-Education of the Sexes in the Public Schools of the U.S.A. (Wash., 1883.)

Smithsonian Institute.

Title and Reports, for 1891, 1892. (Wash., 1892.)

District of Columbia, Washington.

Report of the Commissioners of Education upon the Public Schools of the District of Columbia. (1892.)

Report of the Board of Trustees of the Public Schools of the District of Columbia, 1891–2. (1892.)

Course of Study for the Public Schools of the District of Columbia. (1892.)

Guide to the Student in Botany; Washington High School, by E. S. Burgess.

The Catholic University of America, official announcements. (1892.)

Catalogue of the Mount Vernon Seminary.

School Magazine of   ,,   ,,

Catalogue of Norwood Institute.

School Magazine of   ,,

California, San Francisco.

Board of Education of San Francisco. Report and Bye-laws for 1892.

Revised Course of Study for the Public Schools. (1892.)

Illinois, Chicago.

Annual Report of Board of Education of the City of Chicago for 1890. (1891.)

Rules and Regulations of Board of Education.
Course of Study for High Schools. (1891.)
"White and Blue." Hyde Park High School Magazine for 1892–93.
Quarterly Calendar of the University of Chicago (official), 1892 and 1893.
Programmes of Courses in History, Economics, Natural Science, etc., of University of Chicago. (1892.)
Current Topics, non-official magazine of University of Chicago. Jan. to Oct., 1893.
Course of Study in Cook County Normal School, 1893.

Urbana.

Catalogue of the University of Illinois.

Maryland, Baltimore.

Johns Hopkins University Circular. March, 1893.
Calendar and Regulations of the Woman's College of Baltimore, 1893.
Calendar and Regulations of the Girls' Latin School. (1892.)
Calendar of Bryn Mawr School. 1893.

Massachusetts, Boston.

Annual Report of the Board of Education of Massachusetts for 1891–2. (1893.)
The Public Statutes of Massachusetts relating to Public Instruction, with Annotations and Explanation. (1892.)
Brief Descriptive Sketch of the Mass. Public School System. J. W. Dickinson. (1893.)
Nature Study in the Public Schools of Mass. A. C. Boyden. (1893.)
Calendars of the State Normal Schools. 1892, 1893.
Report of School Committee of Boston. (1893.)
Report of Superintendent of Public Schools. (1892.)
Manual of the Public Schools of Boston. (1893.)
Course of Study, Boston Latin Schools. (1891.)
Description and Dedication of the Girls' High School House. (1872.)
Calendar of the Normal School of Gymnastics. 1892–3.

Programme of the Mass. Institute of Technology for 1892–
1893. (1892.)
Catalogue of Miss Brown's School, Boston.
    „   Lasell Seminary, near Boston.
Report of the Women's Educational and Industrial Union,
Boston.

Brookline.

Town Records and Reports of the Town Officers of Brook-
line for 1892. (1892.)
Report of the School Committee of Brookline for 1892, for
1893. (1892–3.)
Courses of Study issued by the School Committee of
Brookline. 1892, 1893.

Cambridge.

Annual Report of the School Committee, 1891. (1892.)
Appendix to Cambridge School Report. 1890.
Report of the Cambridge Manual Training School for
Boys. (1892.)
Annual Report of the President and Treasurer of Harvard
College. 1891–1892. (1893.)
Harvard University Catalogue. 1892–3. (1892.)
Papers used at the Harvard Examination for Women.
1888, 1890, 1891, 1892.
Report (1891–2) and Courses of Study (1892–3) of the
Society for the Collegiate Instruction of Women.
(1892.)

Northampton.

Official Circular of Smith College for 1892–3. (1893.)

Wellesley.

Wellesley College President's Report. (1892.)
    „   „   Legenda.
    „   „   Calendar.
Dana Hall Circular.

Michigan, Ann Arbor.

Thirty-sixth Annual Report of the Board of Education.
(1892.)
Report of the Superintendent of Public Schools. (1892.)
Catalogues. Ann Arbor High School. 1891–2, 1892–3.

Calendar of the University of Michigan. 1892, 1893.
University Record. April, 1892.
University of Michigan. 1893.
  „   „   „   Commemoration Oration.   1887.
By James P. Angell.   (1888.)

Minnesota, Minneapolis.

Laws of Minnesota relating to the Public School System.
  (1891.)
Seventh Biennial Report of the State Superintendent.
  (1891, 1892.)
Manual of the High School Board, 1891.   (1891.)
Calendar of the University of Minnesota.
Report of the Board of Regents of University of Minne-
  sota for 1891 and 1892.   (1892.)
Seventh Biennial Report of State Normal School Board
  for 1891 and 1892.   (1892.)

New York, Albany.

Publications of the University of the State of New
  York :—
      No. 1. Regents' Bulletins.
       „   2. G. W. Curtis. An Address delivered at
               the University Convocation.   1890.
               (1890.)
       „   4. Regents' Examinations. (1890.)
       „   5. Academic Syllabus. (1891.)
       „   6. Books and Apparatus. (1891.)
       „   8. Report of University Convocation of 1891.
               (18 .)
       „ 11. S. Sherwood.   Origin, History, and
               Present Organization of the University.
               (1893.)
               Regulations of Library and Examinations
               Department. (1893.)
               University Law.   (1893.)

Brooklyn.

Annual Report of the Superintendent of Public Instruction
  to the Board of Education of the City of Brooklyn for
  1892. (1893.)

Course of Study in Mathematics for Primary and Grammar Grades. Brooklyn Board of Education. (1893.)
Examination Papers for Graduation from the Grammar Schools, and for Teachers' Certificates. (Dates various.)
Catalogue for 1893–94. Pratt Institute. (1893.)

New·York.

Board of Education of City of New York. 1891. (1892.)
Reports of the College of the City of New York. 1891–1892, 1892–1893.
Twenty-second Annual Report of the Normal College. (1893.)
Catalogue of Columbia College. 1892–93.
    „   „ Barnard College. 1892-93.
The Year Book. Brearley School. 1892–93.
The Normal College Echo. School Magazine. 1892–93.
Calendars of Dr. Sachs' Collegiate Institute. 1892, 18

Poughkeepsie.

Vassar College Calendar. 1892–93.

Ohio, Cincinnati.

Annual Report of the Public Schools of Cincinnati for 1892. (1893.)

Pennsylvania, Philadelphia.

Seventy-fourth Annual Report of Board of Public Education of the City of Philadelphia for 1892. (1893.)
Annual Report of the Superintendent of Public Schools of the City of Philadelphia for 1892. (1893.)
Report of the Manual Training Schools, Philadelphia, 1893.
University of Pennsylvania Bulletin. April, 1893.
Catalogue of the University of Pennsylvania for 1892–93. (1893.)
Ogontz Mosaic. 1892–93.
Calendar of Friends' Schools, at 15th and Race Streets. (1893.)
Programme of Bryn Mawr College. 1892–93.
Calendar of Swarthmore College. 1892–93.

Virginia, Hampton.

Catalogue of the Hampton Institute. 1891–92.
General Armstrong's Work for Negro and Indian, from
New England Magazine. (Boston, June, 1892.)
The Southern Workman. (Hampton, Nov., 1592.)

Washington, Seattle.

Annual Report of the Board of Education of the City of
Seattle. 1893.

West Virginia, Charleston.

School Law of the State of West Virginia. 1891.
Biennial Report of the State Superintendent of West
Virginia. 1889–90. (1890.)

III.

MISCELLANEOUS WORKS: PAMPHLETS AND PERIODICALS.

W. G. HALE : The Art of Reading Latin. (Boston, 1892.)
Aims and Methods of Classical Study. (Boston,
1892.)
W. T. HARRIS, LL.D. : Lectures on the Philosophy of
Education, given at Johns Hopkins University, Session
1893. (*Educational Times* for July, 1893. London.)
Place of University Extension in American Educa-
tion. (Philadelphia, 1892.)
The Function of the Study of Latin and Greek in
Education. (Pamphlet.)
The Study of Natural Science ; its Uses and Dan-
gers.
Morality in the Schools. (Pamphlet.)
German Instruction in American Schools. (Pam-
phlet.)
B. A. HINSDALE: Topics in the Educational History of
the U.S.A. (Ann Arbor. No date.)
President Eliot on Popular Education. (Pamphlet.)
W. S. JACKMAN: Nature Study for the Common Schools.
(New York, 1892.)
The Relation of Arithmetic to Elementary Science.
(Pamphlet.)
C. F. KING : Methods and Aids in Geography. (Boston,
1889.)

J. MacAlister: Physical Training in Education. (Pamphlet.)

Syllabus of U.S. History and Civil Government. (Philadelphia, 1887.)

The Study of Modern Literature in the Education of our Time. (Pamphlet.)

G. H. Palmer: The New Education. (*Andover Review*, Nov. 1885.)

Possible Limitations of the Elective System. (*Andover Review*, Dec. 1886, Jan. 1887.)

The Glory of the Imperfect. (Boston, 1891.)

G. A. Wentworth: The New Plane and Solid Geometry. (Boston, 1892.)

Proceedings of the Department of Superintendence of the National Educational Association, at its meeting in Philadelphia, 1891. (1891.) In Brooklyn, 1892. (1892.)

Educational Review for 1893. (New York.)

New England Magazine for May, 1893.

    ,,   ,,   ,,   Aug., 1893. (Boston.)

Popular Science Monthly for May, 1893. (New York.)

APPENDIX

TABLE

Shewing *Percentage* of Students in each Subject to *whole number* of Students in Public Secondary Schools for *whole* United States, 1889–1890.

Total number of Students in U.S.A., 202,963.

Branch of Study.	Total No. of Pupils.	Percentage of Pupils.
Latin	70,411	34·69
Greek	6,202	3·05
French. . . .	11,858	5·84
German . . .	21,338	10·51
Algebra . . .	92,150	45·39
Geometry. . .	43,294	21·33
Physics . . .	46,184	22·21
Chemistry . .	20,503	10·10
General History	55,427	27·31
No. of Pupils in whole U.S.A.	202,963	

MASSACHUSETTS SCHOOL LAW.

CHRONOLOGICAL TABLE,

Shewing Increase in the Prescribed or Optional Studies to be taught in Public Schools since 1647.

1647. In Elementary Schools. Reading and Writing required.

  „ Grammar „ To fit for the University.

1789. „ Elementary „ English Language, Arithmetic, Orthography, and Decent Behaviour added.

  Grammar „ To teach Latin, Greek, and English Languages.

1826.	In Elementary Schools.		Geography added.
	„ High	„	History, Algebra, Geometry, Book-Keeping, Surveying, Rhetoric, Logic, Latin, and Greek.
1850.	„ Elementary	„	Physiology and Hygiene made optional.
1857.	„ „	„	United States History added, Algebra made optional.
	„ High	„	Natural Philosophy, Chemistry, Botany, Astronomy, Geology, Civil Polity, Political Economy, Intellectual and Moral Science, and French added.
1860.	„ Elementary	„	Vocal Music and Drawing made optional.
1862.	„ „	„	Agriculture made optional.
1870.	„ „	,	Drawing required.
1876.	„ „	„	Sewing made optional.
1831.	„ „	„	Calisthenics, gymnastics, and Military Drill optional.
1885.	In all Schools		Physiology and Hygiene required.

WELLESLEY COLLEGE.

NUMBER OF STUDENTS ELECTING WORK IN VARIOUS SUBJECTS, 1892.

English Literature	. . . 213	Political Economy.	. . . 22
German	 190	Pedagogics	 20
History	 121	Geology	 16
Greek	 86	Philology.	 16
History of Art	 75	Physiology	 15
French	 74	Physical Astronomy.	. . 14
Latin	 64	Rhetoric	 13
Botany	 53	Bibliography	 11
Chemistry	 50	Domestic Science	 11
Mathematics	 44	Physics	 9
Philosophy	 36	Italian	 7
Elocution	 30	Hebrew	 5
Zoölogy	 28	Entomology	 3

BROOKLINE, MASS.

SUMMARY OF STATISTICS.

Number of Children in town between 5 and 15 years of
age, May 1st, 1892 2,156
Valuation of school buildings and grounds, May 1st,
1891 . . . . $464,509·76
Approximate value of other property, as desks, pianos,
books of reference, etc. . . . . $16,048·00
Assessed valuation of real and personal estates of
Brookline, May 1st, 1892 . . . . $53,080,600·00
Amount expended for support of day schools, in-
cluding repairs . . . . $82,684·03
Additional amount expended for text-books and
supplies . . . . $4,648·67
Total expenditure for the schools for the year, in-
cluding text-books and supplies . . . . $87,857·64
Cost of instruction per pupil, +supplies (books, etc.) . . $38·28
Whole number of different pupils enrolled in all the
schools for the year, including Kindergartens. . . . 2,378
Average whole number for the year. 1,936
Percentage of attendance in all the schools, based on the
average whole number 91
Number of pupils over 15 years of age 250
    „   „   „ between 8 and 14 years of age 1,338
    „   „   „ under 5 years of age 184
    „   „   „ in the High School . . · . . . . . 7·2%
    „   „   „   „ Grammar Schools . . . . . . 46·6%
    „   „   „   „ Primary Schools . . . . . . 34·1%
    „   „   „   „ Kindergartens . . . . 12·1%
Average number of pupils to each teacher—
    in High School 25
    „ Grammar Schools 43
    „ Primary Schools 41
    „ Kindergartens 23
Number of teachers in High Schools 7
    „   „   „ „ Grammar Schools 26
    „   „   „ „ Primary Schools 21
    „   „   „ „ Kindergartens 13
Special Teachers—drawing, 2 ; music, 2 ; sewing, 3 ; cooking,
2 ; carpentry, 2 ; physical culture, 1 ; French, 1 ; sub-
stitute teacher, 1. 14
Total number of teachers in day schools 81

WELLESLEY COLLEGE.

CURRICULUM OF THE CLASSICAL COURSE. (B.A.)

(Required Subjects.)

Freshman Year.	Sophomore Year.	Junior Year.	Senior Year.
Req. No. 15	* 14	15	15
Greek . . . 4	Eng. Literature 1	Logic . . . 2	Rhetoric . 1
Latin . . . 4	Rhetoric . . 1	Rhetoric . . 1	Psychology 3
English . . 1	Chemistry. . 3	History of 2	Bible . . 2
Mathematics 4	Elocution . . 1	European or	
Bible (History	History of	Civilization 3	
of the Jewish	the Jewish	Physics . . 3	
Church) . 2	Church . . 2	Bible . . . 2	
* 15	8	11 or 12	6

* The figures represent the required number of Exercises per week : when the required subjects do not amount to the required number of Exercises, the time must be filled up with Electives, the list of which includes the usual subjects.

BOSTON LATIN SCHOOLS.

COURSE OF STUDY.

Class VI. (lowest) Age 12-13.	Class V. Age 13-14.	Class IV. Age 14-15.	Class III. Age 15-16.	Class II. Age 16-17.	Class I. Age 17-18.
English and History . 6	English and History . 6	English and History . 5	English and History . 4	English and History . 4	English . . 2
Latin . . 5	Latin . . 5	Latin . . 5	French or German . 2	French or German . 2	Physics . . 3½
Geography 2	Geography 2½	French or German . 3½	Latin . . 4	Latin . . 4	Latin . . 4
Elementary Science . ½	Elementary Science . ½	Elementary Science . ½	Greek . . 5	Greek . . 5	Greek . . 4½
Arithmetic 4	Arithmetic 3½	Algebra . 4	Algebra . 3	Algebra and Geometry 3	Geometry . 4
Objective Geometry ½	Objective Geometry ½	Physical Training & Singing . 2	Physical Training & Singing . 2	Physical Training & Singing . 2	Physical Training & Singing . 2
Physical Training & Singing . 2	Physical Training & Singing . 2				
Total hours 20	Total . . 20	Total . . 20	Total . . 20	Total . . 20	Total . . 20

(Some Alternatives allowed according to the College Course for which pupils are preparing.)

SUMMARY OF STATISTICS
OF
PUBLIC AND PRIVATE SECONDARY SCHOOLS IN THE UNITED STATES, 1889–1890.

			Public. Including	Private. Academies.
Number of Schools in 1889–90.			2526	1632
Number of Secondary Instructors	Male . . .		3,597	3,272
	Female . .		5,280	3,937
	Total . .		9,120*	7,209
Number of Secondary Students.	Male . . .		84,451	47,534
	Female . .		116,351	47,397
	Total . .		202,963*	94,931
Number of Coloured Secondary Students	Male . . .		2,512	not given
	Female . .		3,397	
	Total . .		5,933	
No. preparing for College Classical Course	Male . . .		7,984	11,220
	Female . .		6,915	5,429
	Total . .		14,899	16,649
No. preparing for College Scientific Course	Male . . .		6,946	6,326
	Female . .		7,374	3,323
	Total . .		14,320	9,649
No. of Students who have *graduated* or *completed* their studies (1889–90)	Male . . .		7,692	—
	Female . .		14,190	—
	Total . .		21,882	—
Number of *Volumes* in Library . . .			956,832	961,268
Value of ground, buildings, and apparatus.			$49,171,542	$37,521,576
Amount of State and Municipal *Aid* .			$4,354,092	—

* NOTE.—The Figures in the Total Columns do not always represent the addition of the other numbers (Male and Female), as the School Officials in some cases return TOTALS only.

PUPILS.

GENERAL SUMMARY OF ALL GRADES, PUBLIC AND PRIVATE, FOR THE WHOLE UNITED STATES, 1889–90.

Pupils receiving Elementary Instruction :—
Public	12,494,233
Private	1,516,300

Pupils receiving Secondary Instruction :—
Public	221,522
Private	145,481

Pupils receiving Higher Instruction :—
In Universities and Colleges for Men only and Co-educational—

Public (State Universities)	7,071	
Private	39,060	
Total		46,131

In Colleges for Women only—

Private	11,992

Pupils in Normal Schools :—

Public	26,775	
Private	8,189	
Total		34,964

Pupils in Agricultural and Mechanical Colleges	6,349
„ „ Schools of Medicine, Law, and Theology	35,806

WASHINGTON HIGH SCHOOLS.

THREE COURSES OF STUDY OUTLINED.—1892-3.

Year.	Academic.	Scientific.	Business.
FIRST.	English. History. Algebra. Latin. Zoology.	English. History. Algebra. German. Zoology.	English. Business Arithmetic. Book-keeping. Penmanship. Shorthand. *Typewriting* or *Mechanical Drawing.*
SECOND.	English. English History. *Greek.* Geometry. Latin. Physics *or* Chemistry.	English. English History. Geometry. German. Physics *or* Chemistry.	English. Book-keeping and Business Practice. Commercial Law and Commercial Geography. Shorthand and Type-writing. *Mechanical Drawing.*
THIRD.	*Trigonometry* and *Surveying* or *History.* Latin. English. *German. Greek. Botany* or *Chemistry* and *Mineralogy* or *Advanced Physics.*	*Trigonometry* and *Surveying* or *History.* German. English. *Botany* or *Chemistry* and *Mineralogy* or *Advanced Physics.*	Pupils taking this course will attend the Business High School. Each year of this course is complete in itself.
FOURTH.	Latin. English. *Advanced Botany* or *Chemistry* or *Physics. Greek. Geology. History* and *Political Economy. Analytical Geometry* and *College Algebra.*	German. English. *Advanced Botany or* Chemistry *or* Physics. Greek. Geology. *History* and *Political Economy. Analytical Geometry* and *College Algebra.*	

(*a*) Elective studies are *italicised ;* all others are prescribed.
(*b*) Not more than four studies may be pursued at one time.

SMITH COLLEGE.

LITERARY COURSE (B.L.).

| FIRST YEAR. | SECOND YEAR. | JUNIOR YEAR. | SENIOR YEAR. |

FALL TERM.

	Hours.		Hours.		Hours.		Hours.
Greek *or* Latin	3	French	2	French *or*		Pyschology	3
French *or*		German	2	German	2	Political	
German*	4	Rhetoric·		Rhetoric	3	Economy	3
Rhetoric	1	Mechanics				Rhetoric Style	2
Historical	⎫	of Prose					
English,	⎬ 2	and Verse	2				
Prose	⎪	English					
History	⎭	Literature	2				
Hygiene	1	Biblical Study	1				
Lectures on	⎫						
the College	⎪						
and Biblical	⎬ 1						
Study	⎭						

WINTER TERM.

	Hours.		Hours.		Hours.		Hours.
Greek *or* Latin	3	French	2	French *or*		Ethics	3
French *or*		German	2	German	2	Political	
German	4	Old English	1	Logic	3	Science	2
Rhetoric		English		English		Bible Study	1
Verse	1	Literature	2	Literature	2		
English				Biblical Study	1		
Literature	2						
Biblical Study	1						
Elocution	1						

SUMMER TERM.

	Hours.		Hours.		Hours.		Hours.
Greek *or* Latin	3	French	2	French *or*		Evidences of	
French *or*		German	2	German	2	Christianity	2
German	4	History	2	English		Biblical Study	1
Rhetoric		Old English	3	Literature	2		
Verse	1	Bible Study	1	Biblical Study	1		
English							
Literature	2						
Elocution	1						

* The Student will take during this year the language not offered at entrance.

N.B.—Elective work for each year must be selected, under advice of the Class Officers, from the studies offered in the Classical Course.

INDEX.

Academies in New England, 73.

Admission on Certificate, 68.

Age of entering Women's Colleges, 112.

Algebra, 82-4.

American Enthusiasm for Education, 2.

" American Girton," The, 118.

American Ideal of University Education, 105-7.

American Opinion on School Discipline, 61-3.

American School System criticised, 173, 174.

Ann Arbor—Seat of University of Michigan, 142.

Arithmetic, 81, 82.

Art in Women's Colleges, 124, 125, 127.

Astronomy, 87, 103.

Attendance at School, 63.

Bifurcation, 19.

Blackboards, 57.

Boards : Local, their functions, 11 ; State Boards of Education, 13; Local Boards : their defects, 13 ; When they work well, 25 ; Functions in Massachusetts, 30 ; State Boards in Massachusetts, 31 ; High School Boards of Minnesota. 39, 40 ; Central Boards, necessity for, 167 ; Methods of Election, 169.

Boarding Schools for Girls, 75, 76.

Boating at Wellesley, 154.

Boston. High School system, 36 ; Girls' High School Hall, 60; Number of pupils per teacher in High Schools, 70 ; Co-Education in, 160.

Botany, 102, 103.

Boys and Girls in School, compared, 163, 164.

Brookline. Excellence of Schools, 37, 38, 92, 95 ; Science teaching, 100 ; Statistics, Appendix.

Brooklyn High School, 71.

Bryn Mawr. Admission, 68 ; General account, 29 *et. seq.*

Buildings—School, 56, 57; compared with English, 58, 59 ; Women's Colleges, 113, 116.

Bureau of Education, 10.

Cambridge High Schools, 37.

Chemistry, 100, 101.

Chicago, 12.

Chicago University, 27, 133, 134, 135 ; Social life in, 166.

Cities, Great, Schools injured by Politics, 73, 74.

City Organization, 12.

" Civics," 90, 91.

" Class," 48.

Co-Education, 160 *et. seq.* ; in University of Michigan, 141 ; at College, 111, 112.

200

Colleges, 105, 106. *et. seq.*, and Appendix.

College and University, Distinction between, 106.

" Concentration " theory, 96.

Conveyance of pupils to School in Massachusetts, 35.

Cook County Normal School, Chicago, 96, 98, 99.

Corsets forbidden, 158.

Curriculum of Public Schools, 17, 18, 47, and Appendix : Private Schools, 76. College, Appendix.

Daily Routine: High Schools, 50-52 ; Women's Colleges, 113.

Delsarte System, 151, 152.

Degrees, 110, 121, 125, 128, 131.

Discipline in High Schools, 52, 53, its excellence, 61-64, 170.

Drawing, 54.

" Duties of a Citizen," 90.

Elections (mimic) in Schools, 92.

"Electives " at College, 107.

Elementary Education : Statistics 19, and Appendix.

Elocution, 159.

English Language compulsory, 3.

Equality, influence of social equality on Education, 21.

Evening Schools, Massachusetts, 34.

Examinations, 16, 44, 45 ; feeling against, 66-68, 140; unimportant at College, 110.

Fellowships for Women : Bryn Mawr, 130, 172 ; Chicago, 172.

Fees in Private Schools, 75; Women's Colleges, 122, 124, 125, 128, 131.

Flag, National, in Schools, 171.

Finance : cost per child, 14; School Tax, how raised, 14 ; Amount spent, 15 ; Appendix, 6.

Free Schools, 6. 17.

Free Text-Books, 79,

Freedom of Discipline, 52, 63.

Funds, State of, 13, 15 ; in Massachusetts, 32, 33 ; in Michigan, 137, 138.

Furniture, School, 57.

Games not encouraged, 160.

Geometry, 84–87.

German influence on University Education, 137; on physical training, 147.

Girton Students in American Colleges, 130.

Grammar, an Elementary subject, 46 ; see Appendix, School courses.

Grammar Schools, 17, 18.

Greek Art in Schools, 60.

" Group " system at Johns Hopkins', 108 ; Bryn Mawr, 131.

Gymnasia, 59, 153, 156.

Gymnasium costume, 158.

Halls in Schools, 59.

Harvard : Wealth, 2; influence, 27, 41 ; Origin, 28 ; Examination for Women, 67 ; Admission, 68 ; Influence on Science Teaching, 104; Curriculum Elective, 108, 109 ; Physical Training at, 148.

Harvard Annex, its History, work, and Importance, 118 *et. seq.*

Health of School Girls, 55-6. Women at College, 153-5.

Herbart, 9, 72.

High Schools, 46 *et seq.*; Age of Entry, 18 ; Functions, 19 ; in Massachusetts, 36 ; Admission

to, 46 ; Comparison with English,
49, 50 ; High School for Girls,
not public, 73, see also Appendix.
Higher Grade Board Schools.
Equivalent for, 18.
History Teaching, 88 *et. seq.* ;
Important in U.S.A., 89 ; Universal History, 90 ; Illustrations
for Teaching, 96 ; Use of diagrams in Massachusetts Institute, 97 ; Criticism of American
methods, 93, 94.
Holidays, 53.
Home Work, 54, 55.

Kindergartens, 17.

Laboratories, 100, 101.
Languages, Foreign, 22 and Ap-
pendix.
Lectures at College, excessive
number, 115.
Libraries in Schools, 69, 80.
Local Boards of Education, 11
et. seq.

Mann, Horace, 29.
Manual Training, 18, 19.
Marks, 65, 66.
Massachusetts. School Law, 27,
28, 35, and Appendix ; State
Board, 31, 34 ; School Finance,
14 and Appendix.
Massachusetts Institute of Tech-
nology, 112, 132, 133 ; History
at, 97.
Mathematics, 81 *et. seq.*
Matriculation, 112 ; " on Certifi-
cate," 139.
Medical Women and Physical
Training, 149.
Mechanics, 87.
Method, 77 *et. seq.*

Michigan University, 136 *et. seq.*
Minneapolis High School, 101.
Minnesota, Secondary Education
in, 39, 40.
Military Drill for Girls, 147, 158.
Museums at Vassar.
Music, Vocal, in Public Schools, 54,
159 ; Women's Colleges, 124, 125,
127.

National Government in Educa-
tion, 10.
Needlework, 54.
Nervous Tension of American
Life, 148.
" New Education," 8, 9, 98.
New England, township system,
27 ; Influence on U.S.A. in
Education, 27.
New York, Private Schools for
Girls, excellent, 72, 74.
Newspapers in School, 93.
Normal Schools, 71.
Number of Pupils, see Appendix,
15, 20, 70.

Organization of Public Education,
10 *et. seq.*
Original Work in History, 94, 95.
Overwork, 55 ; in Women's Colleges, 115, 116.

Parochial Schools, 73.
Parthenon Frieze in Schools, 60.
Patriotism, Teaching of, 53, 91,
171.
Philadelphia System, 12.
Physics, 100, 101.
Physical Education, 146 *et. seq.*
Politics, Influence of, in Public
Educational System, 13, 26,
168.
Post Graduate Work, 108, 172.

Pratt Institute High School, 92, 93.

Primary Schools, 17.

Private Schools, 72 *et. seq.*; their Function, 72; East and West compared, 73; Preparation for College by, 75, 131; Statistics, see Appendix.

Private Study in Schools, 80.

Public School, Meaning of Term, 17; Classification, 17.

Puritanism and Athletics, 146.

Reading and Writing, 99.

"Recess," 50.

"Recitation," 77, 170.

Recitation Method Discussed, 78, 79.

"Regents" of a University, 43, 44, 137.

Religious Exercises in Public Schools, 50.

Religious Influences in Women's Colleges, 114. 126, 127.

Research, Universities open to Older Women for, 172, 173.

Reports on Pupils, 66.

Salaries low for Women Teachers, 16.

Sanitary Science, 133.

Sanitary Inspection of Schools, 35.

Sargent System of Physical Training, 148–150.

School Law, Sources, 10; Compulsory Subjects in Massachusetts, Appendix.

School Year, 53.

Schoolrooms, 70, 71, 99.

Science in Common Schools, 13, 98, 99, 100; Teaching of, 97 *et. seq.*; in Women's Colleges, 103, 104.

Secondary Education Statistics, 19 and Appendix; Comparison of English and American, 20, 21.

Sectarian Schools, 6, 22, 73.

Self-reliance in American Schools, 81.

Smithsonian Institute, 10.

Social Life in Women's Colleges, 116, 117, 122, 125, 129; in University of Michigan, 141–5.

Southern States, School Finance, 14, 15.

Specialization at College, 107.

State Boards of Education, 13, 31, 39, 40, 167.

State Universities, 43, 136

Statistics, see Appendix.

Superintendents' Work and Qualifications, 23–6; State Superintendents, 13; Rules for, in Massachusetts, 33; Excellence of System, 169.

Swedish System of Gymnastics, 150, 151, 154.

Taxation for School Purposes, 14.

Teachers, 16, 17; Social Position, 1, 5; Men required in Public Schools, 17; Licence to Teach, 24; Removal, 24; Teachers' Institutes, 34; Representation of Teachers on Public Boards, 168.

Teaching, General Method, 78 *et. seq.*

Temperature, 56,

Text-Books, 35, 77, 79.

"Town" (township) System, 30-3; for Statistics see Appendix.

Town and County Councils in Education, 168.

Trigonometry, 87.

Universities, connection with

Secondary Education, 8, 40, 41, 67, 68, 139; Classification of, 41, 42, 105; University of the State of New York, 43–5; Curriculum, 106, 107; Those open to Women, 41, 42, 111; Co-Education in, 165.

Uniformity in Schools of U.S.A., 7.

Unity in American Education, 6, 22.

Vassar, 123–5, 152, 153, 95.

Ventilation, 56.

Wellesley, 126 *et. seq.*, 153–5.

Women's Colleges, Legal Status, 42; Curriculum, 107 and Appendix; Classification, 111; Daily Routine, 112–3; Criticism of, 116–8; Physical Training, 152–9.

Women as Heads of Schools, 16; of Colleges, 128; Teachers in Public Schools, 16, 17; Consideration for Health of Women Teachers in public schools, 55; influence on discipline of Women Teachers, 62; Women admitted to University of Michigan, 141.

Butler & Tanner, The Selwood Printing Works, Frome, and London.

AMERICAN EDUCATION:
ITS MEN, IDEAS, AND INSTITUTIONS
An Arno Press/New York Times Collection

Series I

Adams, Francis. **The Free School System of the United States.** 1875.

Alcott, William A. **Confessions of a School Master.** 1839.

American Unitarian Association. **From Servitude to Service.** 1905.

Bagley, William C. **Determinism in Education.** 1925.

Barnard, Henry, editor. **Memoirs of Teachers, Educators, and Promoters and Benefactors of Education, Literature, and Science.** 1861.

Bell, Sadie. **The Church, the State, and Education in Virginia.** 1930.

Belting, Paul Everett. **The Development of the Free Public High School in Illinois to 1860.** 1919.

Berkson, Isaac B. **Theories of Americanization: A Critical Study.** 1920.

Blauch, Lloyd E. **Federal Cooperation in Agricultural Extension Work, Vocational Education, and Vocational Rehabilitation.** 1935.

Bloomfield, Meyer. **Vocational Guidance of Youth.** 1911.

Brewer, Clifton Hartwell. **A History of Religious Education in the Episcopal Church to 1835.** 1924.

Brown, Elmer Ellsworth. **The Making of Our Middle Schools.** 1902.

Brumbaugh, M. G. **Life and Works of Christopher Dock.** 1908.

Burns, Reverend J. A. **The Catholic School System in the United States.** 1908.

Burns, Reverend J. A. **The Growth and Development of the Catholic School System in the United States.** 1912.

Burton, Warren. **The District School as It Was.** 1850.

Butler, Nicholas Murray, editor. **Education in the United States.** 1900.

Butler, Vera M. **Education as Revealed By New England Newspapers prior to 1850.** 1935.

Campbell, Thomas Monroe. **The Movable School Goes to the Negro Farmer.** 1936.

Carter, James G. **Essays upon Popular Education.** 1826.

Carter, James G. **Letters to the Hon. William Prescott, LL.D., on the Free Schools of New England.** 1824.

Channing, William Ellery. **Self-Culture.** 1842.

Coe, George A. **A Social Theory of Religious Education.** 1917.

Committee on Secondary School Studies. **Report of the Committee on Secondary School Studies, Appointed at the Meeting of the National Education Association.** 1893.

Counts, George S. **Dare the School Build a New Social Order?** 1932.

Counts, George S. **The Selective Character of American Secondary Education.** 1922.

Counts, George S. **The Social Composition of Boards of Education.** 1927.

Culver, Raymond B. **Horace Mann and Religion in the Massachusetts Public Schools.** 1929.

Curoe, Philip R. V. **Educational Attitudes and Policies of Organized Labor in the United States.** 1926.

Dabney, Charles William. **Universal Education in the South.** 1936.

Dearborn, Ned Harland. **The Oswego Movement in American Education.** 1925.

De Lima, Agnes. **Our Enemy the Child.** 1926.

Dewey, John. **The Educational Situation.** 1902.

Dexter, Franklin B., editor. **Documentary History of Yale University.** 1916.

Eliot, Charles William. **Educational Reform: Essays and Addresses.** 1898.

Ensign, Forest Chester. **Compulsory School Attendance and Child Labor.** 1921.

Fitzpatrick, Edward Augustus. **The Educational Views and Influence of De Witt Clinton.** 1911.

Fleming, Sanford. **Children & Puritanism.** 1933.

Flexner, Abraham. **The American College: A Criticism.** 1908.

Foerster, Norman. **The Future of the Liberal College.** 1938.

Gilman, Daniel Coit. **University Problems in the United States.** 1898.

Hall, Samuel R. **Lectures on School-Keeping.** 1829.

Hall, Stanley G. **Adolescence: Its Psychology and Its Relations to Physiology, Anthropology, Sociology, Sex, Crime, Religion, and Education.** 1905. 2 vols.

Hansen, Allen Oscar. **Early Educational Leadership in the Ohio Valley.** 1923.

Harris, William T. **Psychologic Foundations of Education.** 1899.

Harris, William T. **Report of the Committee of Fifteen on the Elementary School.** 1895.

Harveson, Mae Elizabeth. **Catharine Esther Beecher: Pioneer Educator.** 1932.

Jackson, George Leroy. **The Development of School Support in Colonial Massachusetts.** 1909.

Kandel, I. L., editor. **Twenty-five Years of American Education.** 1924.

Kemp, William Webb. **The Support of Schools in Colonial New York by the Society for the Propagation of the Gospel in Foreign Parts.** 1913.

Kilpatrick, William Heard. **The Dutch Schools of New Netherland and Colonial New York.** 1912.

Kilpatrick, William Heard. **The Educational Frontier.** 1933.

Knight, Edgar Wallace. **The Influence of Reconstruction on Education in the South.** 1913.

Le Duc, Thomas. **Piety and Intellect at Amherst College, 1865-1912.** 1946.

Maclean, John. **History of the College of New Jersey from Its Origin in 1746 to the Commencement of 1854.** 1877.

Maddox, William Arthur. **The Free School Idea in Virginia before the Civil War.** 1918.

Mann, Horace. **Lectures on Education.** 1855.

McCadden, Joseph J. **Education in Pennsylvania, 1801-1835, and Its Debt to Roberts Vaux.** 1855.

McCallum, James Dow. **Eleazar Wheelock.** 1939.

McCuskey, Dorothy. **Bronson Alcott, Teacher.** 1940.

Meiklejohn, Alexander. **The Liberal College.** 1920.

Miller, Edward Alanson. **The History of Educational Legislation in Ohio from 1803 to 1850.** 1918.

Miller, George Frederick. **The Academy System of the State of New York.** 1922.

Monroe, Will S. **History of the Pestalozzian Movement in the United States.** 1907.

Mosely Education Commission. **Reports of the Mosely Education Commission to the United States of America October-December, 1903.** 1904.

Mowry, William A. **Recollections of a New England Educator.** 1908.

Mulhern, James. **A History of Secondary Education in Pennsylvania.** 1933.

National Herbart Society. **National Herbart Society Yearbooks 1-5, 1895-1899.** 1895-1899.

Nearing, Scott. **The New Education: A Review of Progressive Educational Movements of the Day.** 1915.

Neef, Joseph. **Sketches of a Plan and Method of Education.** 1808.

Nock, Albert Jay. **The Theory of Education in the United States.** 1932.

Norton, A. O., editor. **The First State Normal School in America: The Journals of Cyrus Pierce and Mary Swift.** 1926.

Oviatt, Edwin. **The Beginnings of Yale, 1701-1726.** 1916.

Packard, Frederic Adolphus. **The Daily Public School in the United States.** 1866.

Page, David P. **Theory and Practice of Teaching.** 1848.

Parker, Francis W. **Talks on Pedagogics: An Outline of the Theory of Concentration.** 1894.

Peabody, Elizabeth Palmer. **Record of a School.** 1835.

Porter, Noah. **The American Colleges and the American Public.** 1870.

Reigart, John Franklin. **The Lancasterian System of Instruction in the Schools of New York City.** 1916.

Reilly, Daniel F. **The School Controversy (1891-1893).** 1943.

Rice, Dr. J. M. **The Public-School System of the United States.** 1893.

Rice, Dr. J. M. **Scientific Management in Education.** 1912.

Ross, Early D. **Democracy's College: The Land-Grant Movement in the Formative Stage.** 1942.

Rugg, Harold, et al. **Curriculum-Making: Past and Present.** 1926.

Rugg, Harold, et al. **The Foundations of Curriculum-Making.** 1926.

Rugg, Harold and Shumaker, Ann. **The Child-Centered School.** 1928.

Seybolt, Robert Francis. **Apprenticeship and Apprenticeship Education in Colonial New England and New York.** 1917.

Seybolt, Robert Francis. **The Private Schools of Colonial Boston.** 1935.

Seybolt, Robert Francis. **The Public Schools of Colonial Boston.** 1935.

Sheldon, Henry D. **Student Life and Customs.** 1901.

Sherrill, Lewis Joseph. **Presbyterian Parochial Schools, 1846-1870.** 1932 .

Siljestrom, P. A. **Educational Institutions of the United States.** 1853.

Small, Walter Herbert. **Early New England Schools.** 1914.

Soltes, Mordecai. **The Yiddish Press: An Americanizing Agency.** 1925.

Stewart, George, Jr. **A History of Religious Education in Connecticut to the Middle of the Nineteenth Century.** 1924.

Storr, Richard J. **The Beginnings of Graduate Education in America.** 1953.

Stout, John Elbert. **The Development of High-School Curricula in the North Central States from 1860 to 1918.** 1921.

Suzzallo, Henry. **The Rise of Local School Supervision in Massachusetts.** 1906.

Swett, John. **Public Education in California.** 1911.

Tappan, Henry P. **University Education.** 1851.

Taylor, Howard Cromwell. **The Educational Significance of the Early Federal Land Ordinances.** 1921.

Taylor, J. Orville. **The District School.** 1834.

Tewksbury, Donald G. **The Founding of American Colleges and Universities before the Civil War.** 1932.

Thorndike, Edward L. **Educational Psychology.** 1913-1914.

True, Alfred Charles. **A History of Agricultural Education in the United States, 1785-1925.** 1929.

True, Alfred Charles. **A History of Agricultural Extension Work in the United States, 1785-1923.** 1928.

Updegraff, Harlan. **The Origin of the Moving School in Massachusetts.** 1908.

Wayland, Francis. **Thoughts on the Present Collegiate System in the United States.** 1842.

Weber, Samuel Edwin. **The Charity School Movement in Colonial Pennsylvania.** 1905.

Wells, Guy Fred. **Parish Education in Colonial Virginia.** 1923.

Wickersham, J. P. **The History of Education in Pennsylvania.** 1885.

Woodward, Calvin M. **The Manual Training School.** 1887.

Woody, Thomas. **Early Quaker Education in Pennsylvania.** 1920.

Woody, Thomas. **Quaker Education in the Colony and State of New Jersey.** 1923.

Wroth, Lawrence C. **An American Bookshelf, 1755.** 1934.

Series II

Adams, Evelyn C. **American Indian Education.** 1946.

Bailey, Joseph Cannon. **Seaman A. Knapp: Schoolmaster of American Agriculture.** 1945.

Beecher, Catharine and Harriet Beecher Stowe. **The American Woman's Home.** 1869.

Benezet, Louis T. **General Education in the Progressive College.** 1943.

Boas, Louise Schutz. **Woman's Education Begins.** 1935.

Bobbitt, Franklin. **The Curriculum.** 1918.

Bode, Boyd H. **Progressive Education at the Crossroads.** 1938.

Bourne, William Oland. **History of the Public School Society of the City of New York.** 1870.

Bronson, Walter C. **The History of Brown University, 1764-1914.** 1914.

Burstall, Sara A. **The Education of Girls in the United States.** 1894.

Butts, R. Freeman. **The College Charts Its Course.** 1939.

Caldwell, Otis W. and Stuart A. Courtis. **Then & Now in Education, 1845-1923.** 1923.

Calverton, V. F. & Samuel D. Schmalhausen, editors. **The New Generation: The Intimate Problems of Modern Parents and Children.** 1930.

Charters, W. W. **Curriculum Construction.** 1923.

Childs, John L. **Education and Morals.** 1950.

Childs, John L. **Education and the Philosophy of Experimental-ism.** 1931.

Clapp, Elsie Ripley. **Community Schools in Action.** 1939.

Counts, George S. **The American Road to Culture: A Social Inter-pretation of Education in the United States.** 1930.

Counts, George S. **School and Society in Chicago.** 1928.

Finegan, Thomas E. **Free Schools.** 1921.

Fletcher, Robert Samuel. **A History of Oberlin College.** 1943.

Grattan, C. Hartley. **In Quest of Knowledge: A Historical Per-spective on Adult Education.** 1955.

Hartman, Gertrude & Ann Shumaker, editors. **Creative Expres-sion.** 1932.

Kandel, I. L. **The Cult of Uncertainty.** 1943.

Kandel, I. L. **Examinations and Their Substitutes in the United States.** 1936.

Kilpatrick, William Heard. **Education for a Changing Civiliza-tion.** 1926.

Kilpatrick, William Heard. **Foundations of Method.** 1925.

Kilpatrick, William Heard. **The Montessori System Examined.** 1914.

Lang, Ossian H., editor. **Educational Creeds of the Nineteenth Century.** 1898.

Learned, William S. **The Quality of the Educational Process in the United States and in Europe.** 1927.

Meiklejohn, Alexander. **The Experimental College.** 1932.

Middlekauff, Robert. **Ancients and Axioms: Secondary Educa-tion in Eighteenth-Century New England.** 1963.

Norwood, William Frederick. **Medical Education in the United States Before the Civil War.** 1944.

Parsons, Elsie W. Clews. **Educational Legislation and Adminis-tration of the Colonial Governments.** 1899.

Perry, Charles M. **Henry Philip Tappan: Philosopher and Uni-versity President.** 1933.

Pierce, Bessie Louise. **Civic Attitudes in American School Text-books.** 1930.

Rice, Edwin Wilbur. **The Sunday-School Movement (1780-1917) and the American Sunday-School Union (1817-1917).** 1917.

Robinson, James Harvey. **The Humanizing of Knowledge.** 1924.

Ryan, W. Carson. **Studies in Early Graduate Education.** 1939.

Seybolt, Robert Francis. **The Evening School in Colonial Amer-ica.** 1925.

Seybolt, Robert Francis. **Source Studies in American Colonial Education.** 1925.

Todd, Lewis Paul. **Wartime Relations of the Federal Government and the Public Schools, 1917-1918.** 1945.

Vandewalker, Nina C. **The Kindergarten in American Education.** 1908.

Ward, Florence Elizabeth. **The Montessori Method and the American School.** 1913.

West, Andrew Fleming. **Short Papers on American Liberal Edu-cation.** 1907.

Wright, Marion M. Thompson. **The Education of Negroes in New Jersey.** 1941.

Supplement

The Social Frontier (Frontiers of Democracy). Vols. 1-10, 1934-1943.